The Joys of Successful Aging *is an eminently readable book
that shines with wisdom, witticism, and biblical illustrations
that everyone of strong faith and advancing years will enjoy.*
—Jesse White, Illinois Secretary of State

*Dr. George Sweeting has written the "classic" on aging suc-
cessfully and joyously. The book has impacted my life deeply
and will do the same for you.*
—Pat Williams, senior vice president of the Orlando Magic

*Only Dr. George Sweeting could make aging attractive
enough to make me wish I were older. This is a treasure trove for
seniors still active in the game of life.*
—Jerry B. Jenkins, author of the Left Behind series
and *Riven*

*My friend Dr. George Sweeting once again shows us the way.
He practices what he preaches, and he's finishing with incredi-
ble style and grace.*
—Dr. Joseph M. Stowell, president,
Cornerstone University

*George Sweeting is ageless! His consistency and character as
well as his intensity and integrity come through on every page
as he helps us all to grow old gracefully.*
—O.S. Hawkins, President/CEO
Guidestone Financial Resources

D1531354

THE JOYS OF SUCCESSFUL AGING

LIVING YOUR DAYS TO THE FULLEST

GEORGE SWEETING

MOODY PUBLISHERS

CHICAGO

All Scripture quotations, unless otherwise indicated, are taken from the
New King James Version. Copyright © 1982 by Thomas Nelson, Inc. Used by
permission. All rights reserved.

Scripture quotations marked NIV are taken from the *Holy Bible, New International Version*®. NIV® Copyright © 1973, 1978, 1984 by International Bible Society. Used by permission of Zondervan. All rights reserved.

Scripture quotations marked NASB are taken from the *New American Standard Bible*®, Copyright © 1960, 1962, 1963, 1968, 1971, 1972, 1973, 1975, 1977,
1995 by The Lockman Foundation. Used by permission. (www.Lockman.org)

Scripture quotations marked KJV are taken from the King James Version.

Editorial services by Julie-Allyson Ieron, Joy Media
Second Edition Editor: Christopher Reese
Interior Design: Ragont Design
Cover Design: Paetzold Design
Cover Image: Comstock

Grateful acknowledgment is hereby expressed to those who have granted
permission to include copyrighted materials in this book. Any inadvertent
omission will be gladly corrected in future editions.

Library of Congress Cataloging-in-Publication Data
Sweeting, George, 1924-
    The joys of successful aging: living your days to the fullest / George
Sweeting.
        p. cm.
    Includes bibliographical references.
    ISBN 978-0-8024-7290-8
    1. Christian aged—Religious life. 2. Aging—Religious aspects—
Christianity. I. Title.

BV4580.S94 2002 248.8'5—dc21

2002070967

We hope you enjoy this book from Moody Publishers. Our goal is to provide
high-quality, thought-provoking books and products that connect truth to your
real needs and challenges. For more information on other books and products
written and produced from a biblical perspective, go to www.moodypublishers.
com or write to:

Moody Publishers
820 N. LaSalle Boulevard
Chicago, IL 60610

1 3 5 7 9 10 8 6 4 2

Printed in the United States of America

THIS BOOK IS AFFECTIONATELY DEDICATED TO OUR GRANDCHILDREN:

Christopher

Erika

Aubrey (deceased)

James

Katelyn

Nathan

Jonathan

Joshua

Jeremiah

Julianna

SPECIAL APPRECIATION IS OFFERED

To my son Dr. Donald Sweeting for reviewing the manuscript and suggesting ways to improve it.

To Dr. Brett Abernathy for reviewing chapters 3, 4, 5, and 6 from his perspective as a medical doctor, a warm thank-you.

To Sarah Abbey for her superb help in preparing this manuscript.

CONTENTS

PREFACE

J oy and aging are seldom linked together; however, I have discovered many unexpected joys as a senior adult.

Through no credit of my own, I was born with a happy disposition. As a child, I must confess I lived on the sunny side of the street. I was a giggler and was occasionally asked to leave the classroom until I could compose myself. Try as I would, when I would reenter the room, the class would erupt in laughter . . . causing me to return to the hallway.

Authentic joy, of course, has nothing to do with brightness of disposition or personality. Authentic joy comes from a spiritual relationship, so that joy is possible even amid earthly limitations and deep sorrow. You *can* age with joy and finish with grace. The word *grace* comes from the Greek word *charis*, suggesting unmerited favor. There are no prerequisites to grace. As Augustine said, "It will not be the grace of God in any way, unless it has been gratuitous in every way."

Caleb, of Old Testament fame, is one of the theme characters of this book. At age eighty-five, when many people dream of retirement, Caleb was going strong. In fact, he claimed to be as strong to serve at age eighty-five as he was at age forty (Joshua 14:11).

Rather than seeking security and ease, he asked for an enemy-infested mountain, so he could give it as an inheritance to his children and grandchildren. Caleb is an authentic role model for all who want to age successfully. His last years were his best . . . and they can be our best, as well.

You and I were created for joy and if we miss it, we miss
the reason for our existence. . . . if our joy is honest joy,
it must somehow be congruous with human tragedy.
This is the test of joy's integrity: is it compatible with pain?
. . . Only the heart that hurts has the right to joy.

—LEWIS B. SMEDES

A chuckle a day may not keep the doctor away,
but it sure does make those times in life's
waiting room a little more bearable.

—ANNE WILSON SCHAEF

When writer Somerset Maugham was recuperating
from the flu, an admirer called and asked,
"Could I send you fruit or would you prefer flowers?"
He was eighty-eight years old. He told her,
"It's too late for fruit, and too early for flowers."

—W. SOMERSET MAUGHAM

If I were given an opportunity to present a gift to
the next generation, it would be the ability
for each individual to learn to laugh at himself.

—CARTOONIST CHARLES SCHULZ

When Michelangelo, already well along in years, was
discussing life with an old friend, the latter commented,
"Yes, after such a good life, it's hard to look death in the eye."
"Not at all!" contradicted Michelangelo.
"Since life was such a pleasure, death coming from
the same great source cannot displease us."

—TEMMLER WERKE

Gentlemen, why don't you laugh? With the fearful
strain that is upon me night and day, if I did not laugh,
I should die. You need this medicine as much as I do.

—ABRAHAM LINCOLN

There is a time for everything, . . .
a time to weep and a time to laugh.

—ECCLESIASTES 3:1, 4 (NIV)

LIGHTEN UP!

T hough the subject of aging is seldom presented with excitement, let alone joy, I have chosen for the sake of encouragement to begin on the lighter side. Humor combats stress and helps us to creatively cope with life. The last years of life can be enjoyable and fulfilling; though I know for some, aging is a challenge.

The simple truth is that aging brings changes including aches and pains; decreased energy; loss of beauty, friends, and family; and greater dependence on doctors and prescriptions. Each of us moves toward physical decline and death. However, our responsibility is to accept aging and seek to maintain the best health we can at any age.

The good news is that we can age productively and successfully and this begins with acceptance.

An aging wife inquired of her husband, "Will you love me when I'm old, gray, and wrinkled?"

To which he answered, "I do."

The newspaper carried this article titled,

HOW TO TELL YOU'RE GETTING OLDER.
You know you're getting older . . .

1. When your knees buckle . . . and your belt won't.
2. When you get into a rocking chair . . . and can't get it rocking.
3. When everything hurts and what doesn't hurt . . . doesn't work.
4. When you bend over to tie your shoelaces and you think . . . Is there anything else I ought to do while I'm down here?
5. When the little old lady you help cross the street . . . is your wife.
6. When year by year your feet seem farther from your hands.
7. When a handsome man or a pretty girl passes . . . and you don't even notice.
8. When, if you're a man, more hair grows out of your ears than on your head.
9. When you stand on one leg . . . and can't get your pants on.
10. When it costs more for your birthday candles . . . than for the cake.
11. When you have so many liver spots on your hand . . . that it looks like speckled sausage.
12. And when you pray for a good prune juice harvest . . . whatever that means.[1]

I was born on October 1, 1924, the same day and year as former President Jimmy Carter. I share the year of my birth so you will know that I too am a senior and have experienced the ups and downs of life. Besides being a senior, twice I have survived cancer. At age twenty, I was told I had testicular cancer and probably wouldn't see the year out. I was told that if I lived, it would be unlikely that I would ever father children. The year was 1944. My doctor was Titus Johnson of Chicago's Swedish Covenant Hospital. Following two surgeries and thirty radiation treatments, I slowly regained my health. During the first two years, I received a thorough physical examination every six months and since then, a yearly checkup. My annual checkup has turned out to be a blessing in disguise, enabling me to catch physical problems in their early stages. And despite Dr. Johnson's predictions, my wife and I were blessed with four sons.

As a teenager, I was naive concerning my health. Sickness taught me to listen to my body. This has been a lifesaver for me. They say if you want to live long, you need to be sick early. Though I'm not sure that's true, my cancer made me aware of my human frailty and also some essentials of good health. I'm sincerely thankful for the life-threatening experience of testicular cancer because of the lessons I learned.

Once again, at age fifty-nine, after a routine transurethral resection of the prostate, cancer cells were discovered. Again, I chose to have thirty radiation treatments. That was over twenty-five years ago, and my present PSA is an amazing .01.

I share this with you first of all because I have learned that cancer . . . does not necessarily mean death. Second, even though I have faced the ravages of disease and pain, through it all I have known a measure of usefulness and much joy. So think of me as an old friend who, having weathered some of the storms of life . . . wants to share some solid encouragement.

USE IT . . . OR LOSE IT

Continual involvement with life is a major requirement for successful aging. It has been said that getting older is like waterskiing: When you slow down, you go down. So . . . keep on going!

The theme of this book is illustrated in the life of Caleb

(Numbers 13–14; Joshua 14). Early in life, he cast his lot with the famous tribe of Judah and was chosen to represent them. He also identified with the minority when ten of the twelve spies brought back a negative report of the Promised Land. Caleb courageously urged the people to "go up at once and take possession" (Numbers 13:30). He told the people not to fear but to move forward. He was *fully involved* at age forty (Joshua 14:7) and fully involved at age eighty-five (Joshua 14:10). In fact, at age eighty-five he displayed the optimism of a twenty-year-old. He professed to be "as strong this day as on the day that Moses sent me" (Joshua 14:11). He was *involved* with life in his youth, during the middle years, and in old age. His *involvement* and *optimism* are two essentials for successful aging.

When the children of Israel conquered the land, Caleb, at age eighty-five, made a megarequest concerning the future: "Now . . . *give me this mountain*. . . . It may be that the Lord will be with me, and I shall be able to drive them out as the Lord said" (Joshua 14:12, italics added). At age eighty-five, Caleb overcame the inhabitants and received Hebron as an inheritance for his children, grandchildren, and great-grandchildren. His last years were his best. Caleb was involved in a cause bigger than himself. Caleb finished with grace.

Until his recent death at age ninety-nine, Dr. Michael DeBakey offered a spectacular example of successful aging. This pioneering heart surgeon had been a leader in his field for more than sixty years. When he was eighty-nine, he supervised open-heart surgery on Boris Yeltsin, then president of Russia.

At an age when many of his contemporaries have given up, he still walked briskly, stood erect, and offered a firm handshake. He maintained a simple lifestyle. He would rise at 5 a.m., eat a light breakfast of fruit, skim the newspaper, and go off to work consulting, reading, evaluating, and offering postoperative care.

He felt the most important steps to successful aging are:

1. **Control hypertension**, which can be done in most cases through medication.
2. **Refrain from smoking**, which is responsible for 20 percent of all deaths from heart disease and 50 percent of all cancer deaths.
3. **Eat a diet low in fat** to reduce the chances of arteriosclerosis and heart disease. (My doctor is fond of reminding me that "In experiments, fat rats die before skinny rats.")

When Dr. DeBakey was asked how he kept active, he answered, "We say of muscles, 'Use it or lose it.' The same thing applies to the mind; the more you use it, the better it functions. It is better to be mentally active than to be a couch potato."[2]

Dr. DeBakey didn't see his passion as the mere extending of life. "The important thing isn't the actual number of years but to function well, both mentally and physically. That's what constitutes life. These people who linger for years, unable to enjoy life—I call that the prolongations of death."[3]

When Dr. DeBakey was twenty-two, as a medical student at Tulane, he invented a roller pump for the propulsion of blood through flexible tubing.

In 1948, while involved in an expanding research career, he was invited to become chairman of surgery at Baylor University, where he built a world-famous hospital as the leading cardiovascular surgeon in the world.

The *American Journal of Cardiology* has recognized him as "the twentieth century's most influential and national medical statesman."

When asked a few years ago what motivates him, his wife Katrina simply answered, "It's love. We live with love." She continued, "Dr. DeBakey is surrounded by the gratitude and love of his patients. This love nourishes and renews him as he continues to serve."

Sherwin Nuland in his book *The Art of Aging* stated, "At ninety-six, DeBakey looked no older than seventy. Though he has not done a whit of fitness exercise since his youth, his five feet ten inches are lean and wiry at 150 pounds."[4]

In an interview for *Esquire* magazine, DeBakey displayed the excitement and vision of a young man. When asked about the future, he answered, "This new century that we're in is going to be one of the most exciting in all history. The medical advances that have taken place since World War II are amazing. I would say this is the best time in the history of the world to be a six-year-old, oh yes. By far, by far."[5]

PEACE AND LOSS

My Scottish mother experienced a lifetime of negatives. Her mother, Annie McKerrow Irving, died giving birth to her third child, leaving her husband, George Irving, to care for my mother, her brother, Isaac, and the newborn, Annie.

Life was hard in their Carstairs Junction home in Scotland. Her father found it impossible to work and handle his three young children as a single parent. At first, he hired a live-in housekeeper who, along with her children, moved in. Eventually, George Irving married a widow with three children and brought them into the household. However, daily living was so stressful that my mother's brother, Isaac, at fourteen, left home and joined the British navy, while her sister, Annie, ran away, never to be heard from again.

Though my mother's childhood included great sorrow, she experienced a marvelous change in her teens. An acquaintance, Jesse Kay, whom I met decades later, began a girls club in Carstairs Junction. After several visits to the club, my mother,

Mary Rodger Irving, experienced a spiritual awakening. As a teenager, she blossomed into a bright, winsome, and committed Christian. Her faith made her home situation tolerable.

My father, William Sweeting, after returning from fighting three years in Belgium in World War I with the Royal British Engineers, picked up his trade as a stonemason. His work brought him to Carstairs Junction, where he helped build a large stone bridge over the town's railroad station. There my parents met. My mother quickly shared her faith, telling of her life's transformation. She also urged my father to visit two centers in Glasgow, called Bethany Hall and Tent Hall, where he could hear more about the new life she had discovered.

Because of my father's war experience and dissatisfaction with life in general, he was eager to visit Bethany Hall, where he also experienced a spiritual transformation. The change in his life was so dramatic that his father feared he would become a fanatic. His conversion led to eventual courtship and marriage to my mother, Mary Rodger Irving of Carstairs Junction, in 1920.

Tired of Europe's wars and eager to better themselves, they immigrated to the United States in 1923.

Though my father was the unquestioned head of the home, my mother was "the heart of the home." Along with a sincere faith, she possessed a loving, cheerful disposition. She gave birth to six children: William, Anne, George, Norman, Mary, and Martha.

In the 1940s, she was afflicted with rheumatoid arthritis. At times, her condition was so severe that she was bedfast for months and even years. Her hands were deformed and her joints gnarled, yet even in suffering she was attractive. With the advent of cortisone, she managed with great difficulty to get about the home.

Her faith was obvious to all who came to visit. Amid constant pain and meager assets, she displayed a joyful spirit and a gentle sense of humor during forty years of suffering. Her winsomeness in suffering was not due to her personality but the result of trust. She believed that if God allowed suffering, He would give equal grace. I saw firsthand that it is possible . . . amid suffering . . . to age with joy and finish with grace.

Psalm 92:12–15 (NIV) offers an upbeat picture of aging.

> The righteous will *flourish* like a palm tree, they will grow like a cedar of Lebanon; planted in the house of the Lord, they will *flourish* in the courts of our God. They will *still bear fruit in old age, they will stay fresh and green, proclaiming,* "The Lord is upright." (emphasis added)

To *flourish* means to thrive . . . to blossom . . . to abound! The word *abound* comes from the Latin, meaning to overflow, like a cresting, incoming sea wave, splashing in every direction. Seniors are also compared to attractive palm trees and towering cedars. The psalmist declares, "They will still bear fruit in old age." That speaks of continued usefulness. I find joy in the statement, "They will stay fresh and green." This suggests zest, optimism, vitality, and participation in all of life.

Comedian Woody Allen once quipped, "Eighty percent of success in life is in showing up." Well, showing up *is* very important, but CONTINUED INVOLVEMENT with life, amid pain and loss, is all-important to successful aging.

So keep on keeping on. Use it . . . or lose it! Keep involved even amid your tears, and don't take yourself too seriously. Lighten up . . . and keep climbing!

MOTHER TO SON, 1926

Well, son, I'll tell you:
Life for me ain't been no crystal stair.
It's had tacks in it,
And splinters,
And boards torn up,
And places with no carpet on the floor—
Bare.
But all the time
I'se been a-climbin' on,
And reachin' landin's,
And turnin' corners,
And sometimes goin' in the dark
Where there ain't been no light.
So boy, don't you turn back.
Don't you set down on the steps
'Cause you finds it's kinder hard.
Don't you fall now—
For I'se still goin', honey,
I'se still climbin',
And life for me ain't been no crystal stair.

—LANGSTON HUGHES
(African-American writer, 1902–1967)

Anybody who can still do at sixty . . . what he was
doing at twenty. . . wasn't doing much at twenty.

—FORMER PRESIDENT JIMMY CARTER

———

"I don't feel like an old man, I feel like a young man . . .
who has something the matter with him.

—BRUCE BLIVEN

———

THE LITTLE BOY AND THE OLD MAN (1981)

Said the little boy, "Sometimes I drop my spoon."
Said the little old man, "I do that too."
The little boy whispered, "I wet my pants."
"I do that too," laughed the little old man.
Said the little boy, "I often cry."
The old man nodded, "So do I."
"But worst of all," said the boy, "it seems
Grown-ups don't pay attention to me."
And he felt the warmth of a wrinkled old hand.
"I know what you mean," said the little old man.

—SHEL SILVERSTEIN

———

The positive benefits of religion in the lives of elderly adults
are many. Researchers at Georgetown University reviewed
over 200 studies of religion and health. They found that three-
fourths of the studies revealed the positive effects of religion
on drug abuse, depression, blood pressure, and heart disease.
Other researchers have found that the greater the religious
involvement of elderly people, the greater their self-esteem.

—DONALD H. KAUSLER AND BARRY C. KAUSLER

Chapter 2

PEOPLE OF FAITH TEND TO LIVE LONGER

While I was appearing on a talk show with educators and clergy, the host read a quotation from *USA Today* claiming that people of religious faith tend to live longer than people of no faith. The host, though skeptical, asked if there was any validity to such a statement. Because I had read the same article and felt the statement was valid, I volunteered to respond. The moderator pointed at me and said, "Elucidate." I proceeded to give five reasons why I agreed.

1. PEOPLE OF FAITH VIEW THE PHYSICAL BODY AS GOD'S TEMPLE.

People of the Judeo-Christian faith believe all men and women are created in the image of God (Genesis 1:27). They also embrace the words of the psalmist, "You have made him a little lower than the angels, and You have crowned him with glory and honor" (Psalm 8:5). The New Testament also teaches that the human body is "the temple of God" (1 Corinthians

3:16–17) and should not be defiled. In fact, neglect of the body insures a divine penalty (1 Corinthians 3:17).

Comedian Bill Cosby occasionally refers to physical fitness as "temple keeping" and I understand why. Our bodies are special gifts that are viewed as sacred.

Other religious faiths also hold a high view of the body and, for the most part, consider the body a divine gift. If people believe God dwells in them, it makes a megadifference in how they treat their bodies.

Decades before the surgeon general warned of the dangers of tobacco, millions of people of faith abstained from smoking because they felt tobacco was harmful to the body. This application was also made to drugs in general. It extended to moderation in eating, sleeping, and life as a whole. Granted, some carried these prohibitions to extremes; however, in general, they were reasonably applied.

According to a Gallup Poll, 85 percent of those who responded believe physical health depends largely on how people care for their bodies. In other words, the individual makes a contribution to good health. We choose to treat the body with care and respect, *especially* if we believe the body is *sacred*. For this reason alone, people of faith tend to live longer.

2. PEOPLE OF FAITH ULTIMATELY TRUST GOD.

This mind-set is expressed in phrases like, "God willing" or "if God wills." People of faith are encouraged to commit everything in life to a caring, all-wise, all-powerful God. In other words, sufficient grace will be given for whatever He allows. National polls affirm that 80 percent of people over age sixty-five claim that religious beliefs are important in their lives.

Life, though enjoyable, isn't easy. In fact, life is difficult. However, people of faith don't live life alone. They find strength in words like, "O Lord, You have searched me and known me

. . . and are acquainted with all my ways" (Psalm 139:1, 3). Or, "all things work together for good to those who love God, to those who are the called according to His purpose" (Romans 8:28). Promises like these enable people to transcend the limitations and losses of life.

Joseph, of the Old Testament, illustrates this attitude of trust. As a boy he dreamed of future greatness, even though his dreams did not include the hardships he would endure before he would experience greatness. Joseph's brothers hated him because of his dreams of superiority and eventually sold him to some Midianites (Genesis 37:27–28). In Egypt, he gradually achieved success in the house of Potiphar, only to be abused by his employer's wife. This was followed by banishment to a dungeon for thirteen years.

Despite huge obstacles, Joseph believed God was in charge and that even his troubles were part of a divine preparation for future success and leadership. Ultimately, Joseph was reunited with his brothers. In the meantime, he had risen to become leader of Egypt, second only to Pharaoh. When Joseph met his brothers, they fell before him in terror. Then Joseph said to them, "You meant evil against me; but God meant it for good, in order to bring it about as it is this day, to save many people alive" (Genesis 50:20). Joseph's faith in God sustained him for a lifetime and enabled him to survive.

Likewise, on November 21, 2001, *USA Today* recalled Lisa Beamer's faith in the light of the crash of Flight 93, September 11, 2001.

> Terrorists took Lisa Beamer's husband from her, but she refuses to forfeit her zest for life or faith in God.
> She lost her husband Todd, after he and others on Flight 93 battled hijackers for control of their plane. Although it crashed, killing all 44 aboard, the aircraft never hit its Washington, D.C., target.

Now Beamer, mother of two small boys and expecting again in January, is determined to see that terrorists also miss the mark to wreck her life and the future of the children whose parents perished on the plane.

Speaking of her husband's death, Lisa said, *"God ultimately has a plan. He takes us where we need to be."*[1]

People of faith, though not exempt from tragedy, ultimately commit their struggles to a sovereign God who is in charge of all of life. Often I have quoted, "It is vain for you to rise up early, to sit up late, to eat the bread of sorrows; for . . . He gives His beloved sleep" (Psalm 127:2).

Dr. David Snowdon in his book *Aging with Grace* describes his careful study of an order of nuns and applies his findings to what we can learn about health and longevity. Though he freely admits this can't be scientifically tested, after years of observation he attributes their vigor, good health, and longevity to their faith, which serves as a shield against the inevitable tragedies of life.[2] Snowdon also believes there is growing evidence of the value of prayer, meditation, and faith as it relates to aging.

Herbert Benson of Harvard Medical School has written that frequent prayer can reduce pain in cancer patients and even lower blood pressure.[3]

3. PEOPLE OF FAITH ARE PART
OF A LARGE EXTENDED FAMILY.

Loneliness is the first thing God called "not good" in the book of Genesis, and yet it is part of human experience. Loneliness is defined as a feeling of separation, isolation, and distress. As Donald and Barry Kausler explain, the elderly are particularly vulnerable to these feelings.

A Harris survey revealed that the proportion of elderly people experiencing loneliness is substantial. In fact, loneliness is ranked high among the most serious problems older people believe to confront them. . . . The probable causes of loneliness for elderly people were investigated by researchers at the University of South Carolina. Information was obtained from nearly 3,000 individuals aged 65 and older. A number of conditions were found to contribute to loneliness experienced by many elderly people. However, the most important contributor was a low level of social fulfillment. Reduced social fulfillment means that they do not have enough to do to keep busy, and they do not feel needed. Among the other conditions contributing to loneliness of elderly people are changed marital status, reduced income, anxiety, frequency of telephone contact, and poor health. However, the effects of these other contributors are largely indirect: that is, they affect loneliness largely by way of their negative influences on social fulfillment.[4]

Loneliness exists in part because life is a journey. In his well-known classic work *The Confessions of St. Augustine,* Augustine wrote, "You have made us for Yourself, and our hearts are restless until they find peace in You."

An older friend said, "I'm not afraid of dying, but I am afraid of living 'til I die."

The brilliant Albert Einstein, speaking of loneliness, said, "It's strange to be known universally, and yet to be so lonely." Though people of faith experience loneliness as well, it is possible for them to enjoy the support and relationship of a worldwide spiritual family of like-minded people. This oneness is further experienced in local church gatherings where the members are much like family. People need people, and the lack of relationship kills. Centenarians are almost never "loners."

Loneliness appears to attract illness and in some cases even promotes early death.

David Snowdon in *Aging with Grace* speaks forcibly about the strength of community in the nuns' study.[5]

In general, people connected with others through marriage, friendships, clubs, teams, and especially houses of worship live longer. People of faith are not only part of a megahuman family, but they are also related to a universal spiritual family.

We never outgrow our need for others. In fact, giving ourselves to help others is even more life building than receiving help from others. The law of living is . . . giving.

4. PEOPLE OF FAITH CONTINUE THEIR INVOLVEMENT WITH LIFE IN THEIR PLACES OF WORSHIP.

In a seven-year study of seniors by the Center for Health Sciences/Institute for the Study of Human Knowledge, religious involvement was linked to less physical disability and less depression. A variety of studies suggest that religious belief and practice is also associated with less risk of self-destructive behaviors (smoking, drug and alcohol abuse, suicide), less perceived stress, and greater overall life satisfaction.

Involvement with people of all ages in a local place of service is life building and life extending. Places of worship have more individuals serving in their senior years than any other organizations. Claude Pepper, onetime representative for the state of Florida and onetime chairman of the House Select Committee on Aging, commented that "life is riding a bicycle. You don't fall off unless you stop pedaling."

So keep pedaling. Keep involved. Activity is crucial. Seniors need to be pushed to stay involved. Involvement with all ages of people is a major factor in successful aging.

5. PEOPLE OF FAITH TEND TO LIVE LONGER SPECIFICALLY BECAUSE OF THEIR FAITH.

Caleb, our theme person, exemplifies at least three longevity traits, but none more than his dynamic faith. (Chapter 9 will explore this in greater detail.)

In *The Graying of America,* the authors ask,

> Does religion actually serve to improve the health of elderly people? Over 10 years of studies at various university hospitals has indicated that, regardless of the nature of a person's religious preference, people who have a deep religious faith seem to get sick less often and get better faster when they do get sick than people with much less religious faith. Those with a strong religious faith have also been found to have lower rates of heart disease, stroke, and cancer. . . . The higher survival rate for frequent church attenders was especially characteristic of women, but it did apply to men as well. Most important, the difference in survival rates held up even after controlling for differences between frequent and less frequent attenders in health and health practices. Not surprisingly, about 30 of the 125 accredited medical schools in the United States have included religious or spiritual teaching in their curricula.[6]

Others also affirm the results of faith on good health and healing. Dr. Herbert Benson, of Harvard Medical School, speaks of the Faith Factor. He highlights this in his book *Beyond the Relaxation Response* as a means of natural healing that results from:

1. A strong personal belief system that accepts the importance of caring for the body, and

2. The practice of prayer and meditation as part of those beliefs.[7]

Overwhelming evidence points to a strong relationship between faith and good health.[8]

I have used the phrase "people of faith" as it applies to all people who hold deep religious beliefs. However, as a Christian minister and educator for six decades, faith for me has its roots in the Bible, the inspired Word of God.

At this point, because I had consumed most of the airtime, the moderator lifted his hands in a gesture of surrender, saying, "You've made a believer out of me!"

Dr. Andrew Weil, M.D., writes, "To age gracefully means to let nature take its course while doing everything in our power to delay the onset of age-related disease, or, in other words, to live as long and as well as possible, then have a rapid decline at the end of life."[9]

Chapter 3 tells how to keep our bodies healthy so that our last years can be productive.

My son, do not forget my teaching,
but keep my commands
in your heart, for they will prolong your
life many years and bring you prosperity.
Let love and faithfulness never leave you;
bind them around your neck, write
them on the tablet of your heart.
Then you will win favor and a good name
in the sight of God and man.
Trust in the Lord with all your heart and lean
not on your own understanding; in all
your ways acknowledge him,
and he will make your paths straight.
Do not be wise in your own eyes; fear
the Lord and shun evil. This will bring health
to your body and nourishment to your bones.

—PROVERBS 3:1–8 (NIV)

The good news is that moderate, regular exercise has many of the benefits of more strenuous athletics. The bad news, all too familiar, is that most older men and women do not engage even in moderate exercise on a regular basis.

—JOHN W. ROWE AND ROBERT L. KAHN

The cure for age is interest, enthusiasm, and work. Life's evening will take its character from the day which has preceded it. You will always find joy in the evening . . . if you've spent the day well.

—GEORGE MATHESON

The scientists identified maintenance of physical activity throughout life and maintenance of social and intellectual connectedness as the two outstanding common features of the lifestyles of their subjects.

—ANDREW WEIL, M.D.

To keep your brain young and protect yourself from age-related cognitive decline, learn to use a computer if you do not now use one, change your operating system frequently, and learn another language. By the way, I am not at all convinced that cognitive decline is an inevitable consequence of aging. Rather, I think most people simply do not give themselves the kind of mental challenges that brains need to retain their functionality.

—ANDREW WEIL, M.D.

Do you not know that your body is a temple of the Holy Spirit, who is in you, whom you have received from God? You are not your own; you were bought at a price. Therefore honor God with your body.

—1 CORINTHIANS 6:19–20 (NIV)

Chapter 3

TEMPLE KEEPING

C omedian Bill Cosby, in his best-selling book *Time Flies*, enthusiastically shares some of his aging stories. He begins, "Temple was not just my college but a description of my body as well."

Being a native of Philadelphia and a former student of Temple University, he tells how his onetime muscular, sleek body began to resemble his father's size and shape. Wistfully he asks, "What had happened to the temple?" He concludes that his body was being vandalized by time and attacked by an enemy called aging.

I laughed as Cosby described the ritual of taking his shoes off and praying for "longer arms" so that he wouldn't feel like he was about to give birth. With great humor he watches his body change from "a temple" to what he calls, "a storefront church."[1]

People of faith believe that men and women are made in the image of God (Genesis 1:26–27). Some of us go further and claim that the body is specifically "the temple of God," and

God's Spirit indwells it. If this is so, then there are enormous implications concerning how the body is treated. The apostle Paul reminds the people of the city of Corinth, "You were bought at a price. Therefore *honor God with your body*" (1 Corinthians 6:20 NIV, italics added).

Temple keeping includes a broad spectrum of stewardship. However, I will highlight three areas: eating, exercise, and emotions.

YOU ARE WHAT YOU EAT

That was the title of a book I read in the 1960s. Though I have forgotten much of its information, I began to look at what I ate as essential to good health. Recent years have affirmed the fact that our eating habits are either life building or life destroying. After analyzing a sizeable amount of scientific evidence, the American Heart Association concludes that *eating right is essential to good health.* It claims what we eat plays a major role in whether or not we will develop certain types of cancer.

There are many choice books by experts on the subject of eating. Many of them offer similar kinds of advice. For example, authorities advocate that we:

1. Drink plenty of water each day. At least a quart but preferably two quarts of water per day. It's the best drink around. It gives a feeling of fullness with no calories. "Older people, on the average, need six to eight cups of water per day to maintain normal body functions."[2]
2. Eat foods low in fat and cholesterol.
3. Eat more high-fiber foods, as experts tell us they appear to lower cholesterol.
4. Eat lots of fruits and vegetables.

5. Limit your consumption of salt. The average person consumes twenty times more sodium than the body needs.
6. Aim for your proper body weight. As a rule, overweight people die before those who maintain a proper body weight.

These suggestions apply to everyone but especially to those who view the body as God's dwelling place. Eating right is wise temple keeping.

WALK FOR YOUR LIFE

The story is told of two farmers out for a morning walk when suddenly a black bear appeared behind them. One farmer quickly sat down and put on his running shoes. The other farmer laughed at him and mocked, "You can't outrun that bear!" "No," answered the other farmer, "but I can outrun you!"

Webster defines *exercise* as "bodily exertion for keeping the organs and functions healthy." In 1996, the surgeon general included inactivity as a risk factor for premature death and disability.

The fact is, exercise slows time down. Seniors need to be encouraged and even pushed to exercise as much as possible.

According to Donald H. Kausler and Barry C. Kausler, "Millions of older men won't eat vegetables, won't exercise, and won't participate in a senior health promotion program. Nor do older men visit a physician as often as older women do. When they do see a physician, they ask fewer questions and seek less information than older women do. Many older men see themselves as being self-reliant. Seeing a physician may be viewed as a sign of weakness."[3]

Moderate exercise can produce dramatic results in overall good health. Mayo Clinic has prepared a booklet titled *Walk Your*

Way to Fitness, which states, "A brisk walk, thirty to sixty minutes each day, can help you live a longer, healthier life . . . Exercise doesn't have to be a high-intensity activity. Even walking slowly can lower your risk of heart disease. Walking faster, farther, and more frequently offers even greater health benefits."

In 1998, John W. Rowe, M.D., and Robert L. Kahns, Ph.D., wrote *Successful Aging*, a summary of the MacArthur Foundation Study of Aging in America. Sixteen scientists from different fields collaborated on this project, which included studies of over a thousand well-functioning older people. The scientists identified maintenance of physical activity throughout life and maintenance of social and intellectual connectedness as the two outstanding common features of the lifestyles of their subjects. These characteristics were more prominent than any particular dietary patterns or the use of dietary supplements.[4]

My wife and I are avid walkers. On excessively hot or stormy days, we walk at a mall before the shoppers arrive. After thirty or forty minutes, we sit for a casual glass of juice or a fruit cup. We began several decades ago and attempt to walk a minimum of two miles per day, four or five days a week. I began walking as a stress reliever and found it helped me cope with the pressures of work. Walking also enhances sleep. In fact, if I do not walk or work in the garden, my sleep is significantly impaired. Walking for me is the key to every other activity; however, it requires discipline.

Walking also sharpens and stimulates the mind. Some of my best ideas for writing and speaking have come to me as I walked. Frankly, I can't afford not to walk. I walk for my life. For me, walking is a part of temple keeping. I walk to honor God.

EMOTIONS

Worry, fear, and depression are emotions common to all. General Ulysses S. Grant tells in his memoirs how he had become dizzy and could not see well because of violent headaches. His entire body ached. Then one morning a horseman galloped up to him with a note of surrender from General Robert E. Lee of the Confederate army. Grant said, "I was instantly cured when I saw the contents of the note. Every pain immediately left me; even my headache." Grant had been sick from worry.

In spring 1871, a young man picked up a book and read twenty-one words that changed his life. The young man was a medical student at the Montreal General Hospital. He was worried about final examinations. Larger worries also bothered him. He was troubled about what he should do with his life, where he should establish his medical practice, and how he would build it.

The twenty-one words that changed his life were written by Thomas Carlyle. The man who was challenged was William Osier, a founder of Johns Hopkins School of Medicine. Here are the twenty-one words:

> *Our main business is not to see*
> *What lies dimly at a distance but*
> *To do what lies clearly at hand.*[5]

This idea is taught in the Lord's Prayer. "Give us *this day* our daily bread" (Matthew 6:11, italics added). Notice the words "this day." The prayer asks for today's bread only. It doesn't complain about yesterday's bread; nor does it worry about the bread for the next week or next month. The focus is on "this day." Worry doesn't solve tomorrow's problems, but it does ruin today's happiness.

Today's bread is the only bread we can eat. This is what Matthew 6:34 (NIV) states: "Do not worry about tomorrow, for tomorrow will worry about itself. Each day has enough trouble of its own."

Worry winds us up and also wears us down. "Died of worry" could be written on thousands of tombstones. Worry leads to loss of power to will. When we worry, we become so divided that it is difficult to act in a single direction or even make the smallest decision.

Unfortunately, worry is a leading ailment in our world, and it's contagious. Charles Haddon Spurgeon, a nineteenth-century London minister, relates how he worried for weeks before a speaking engagement, even to the extent of hoping he would break a leg before the particular occasion. The result was that when it was time to speak, he was exhausted from worry.

Then Spurgeon faced up to the situation. He asked, "What is the worst thing that could happen to me during my address?" Whatever it was, he decided, the heavens would not fall. He recognized that he had been magnifying his fears. When he faced his worries for what they were, he relaxed, simply because his mind was no longer divided.

General Douglas MacArthur said in 1945: "You don't get old from living a particular number of years; you get old because you have deserted your ideals. Years wrinkle your skin, renouncing your ideals wrinkles your soul. Worry, doubt, fear, and despair are the enemies that slowly bring us down to the ground and turn us to dust before we die."

IS THERE A CURE FOR WORRY?

Consider Prayer

Luke 18:1 (KJV) reads, "Men ought always to pray, and not to faint." Prayer is God's way to keep us from falling apart.

September 11, 2001, may have been one of the bloodiest days in U.S. history when two of our biggest office towers were destroyed and the Pentagon, a symbol of American military authority, was torn apart like an egg carton. In the aftermath of this attack, millions of people turned to prayer.

Alfred Tennyson wrote, "More things are wrought by prayer than this world dreams of." Prayer is one of God's cures for worry.

The psalmists tell us to bring our fears to God in faith. "Trust in the Lord, and do good" (Psalm 37:3). Fear creates friction but no forward progress. Fretting heats the axle but fails to generate forward movement. In a real sense, worry is a form of atheism because it closes our eyes to God's active concern and care.

It is often helpful to make a list of what worries you. As you list the items, you may discover many are vague and unnecessary.

Consider Work

Psalm 37 suggests, "Trust in the Lord, and *do good*" (italics added). The best cure for worry is *work*. "It is not work that kills men," wrote Henry Ward Beecher. "It is worry. Work is healthy. . . . Worry is rust on the blade." Work makes the day go faster. There are days when I do not feel good *until* I become fully involved in some project. Work is a vital part of being alive. Positive work on behalf of others is one of the best ways to overcome worry. Though we do not engage in works for God's acceptance, the Bible urges all "to be ready for every good work" (Titus 3:1).

Suppose a group of vandals broke into your local place of worship and smashed the stained glass windows, splintered the pews, and stained the carpets. You would be offended and rightly so. Desecrating a house of worship is a serious matter. Yet it is far more tragic to vandalize the human body, God's temple, through worry, unnecessary fear, inactivity, and poor eating habits. Temple keeping is strategic to successful aging.[6]

Old people are our links to our history.
As you age your worth in this respect increases.

—Andrew Weil, M.D.

———

To me, old age is fifteen years older than I am.

—Bernard Baruch

———

A stock broker urged Claude Pepper to buy stock that would triple in value every year. Pepper replied, "At my age, I don't even buy green bananas."

—Claude Pepper

———

Old people are survivors, who have avoided the pitfalls of reckless youth and avoided the common failings of middle age. I do not regard their white hair and wrinkled faces as signs of frailty or detractions from human beauty. I see these features as the banners of survivorship.

—Andrew Weil, M.D.

———

Popular wisdom is right when it asserts that money is not everything. The doctor has enough experience of people to realize that. He sees very unhappy people among those who are very wealthy, and others who suffer terribly from boredom amidst their expensive amusements. All the same, there is a threshold below which the condition of the pensioner is deplorable. Everything that one can write on the problems of retirement will be no more than words in the wind or "a cymbal clashing" (1 Cor. 13:1), in St. Paul's words, if a radical change is not made in the financial situation of the low-income pensioner.

—Paul Tournier

Chapter 4

THE AGE BOOM

There's no doubt about it, our world is experiencing a phenomenon like no other in recorded history. Peter G. Peterson, chairman of the Blackstone Group and advisor to presidents, says, "Global aging will become the transcendent political and economic issue of the twenty-first century."[1]

Because of the advances in medicine, science, nutrition, and health awareness, most people will live longer than they expected. Retirement could well be deferred to age seventy or even eighty while others may choose to pursue new careers several times. In the past, long life was the exception rather than the rule.

In 1776, when the United States became an independent nation, a person could expect to live about thirty-five years, even though the median age of the population was sixteen. By 1876, there was a modest improvement and life expectancy was forty, while the median age was twenty-one. The high death rate and high birthrate helped keep America young. It's interesting to visit the graves of historic cemeteries and realize many of the soldiers were between fifteen and twenty-five years of age.

The builders of the railroads and canals were also young people, often immigrants seeking a better life. My parents left Scotland for America while still in their twenties. My wife's parents likewise emigrated from Germany while still in their twenties.

CAUSES OF THE AGE BOOM

The astounding breakthroughs in health care, along with the reduction or elimination of death-causing diseases, appear to be the major reasons for our present age boom. For example, my mother's mother died while giving birth to her third child because of a breech birth. Today, such a birth can be predicted, and both mother and child are likely to survive.

My childhood playmate's father died from tuberculosis before age thirty. Several grade school playmates died from pneumonia. My three sisters and two brothers experienced an array of childhood diseases from scarlet fever to measles. My older brother nearly died at age fourteen from a streptococcus infection. The dreaded disease of the 1930s was poliomyelitis; however, with the arrival of the Salk vaccine, this scourge has been almost eradicated. Scores of life-threatening diseases have been practically removed.

Science and medicine have added approximately twenty-eight years of life to the average person since the early 1900s. A child born today in the United States has a life expectancy of approximately seventy-five years. The National Bureau of Aging projects that by 2040 men will probably live an average of eighty-six years and women about ninety-two years.

Many nations are building a society of active, involved, and relatively healthy seniors. And yet we all age. The fact is that everything in the universe ages.

In his book *The Virtues of Aging,* former President Carter reminds us that Americans over age sixty-five outnumber teenagers. He also says that during the past twenty-four years those over eighty-five grew at a pace about six times greater than the overall population, and—get this—those over one hundred years of age are the fastest-growing group of all. In 1956, there were 2,500 centenarians, 25,000 in 1986, and 268,000 in the year 2000. It is estimated that by the year 2050 there will be 600,000 centenarians in the United States alone. No wonder Hallmark has prepared a special line of cards for this group.

WHERE PEOPLE LIVE LONGEST

The age boom is a worldwide phenomenon with thirteen countries possibly surpassing the United States in longevity. According to the U.S. Bureau of the Census (1987), here are the twenty most longevous countries (listed by percent of population over age sixty-five):

1. Sweden / 18%
2. Norway / 16%
3. United Kingdom / 15%
4. Denmark / 15%
5. Switzerland / 15%
6. Austria / 15%
7. Germany / 15%
8. Belgium / 14%
9. Italy / 14%
10. Greece / 14%
11. Luxembourg / 14%
12. France / 13%
13. Finland / 13%
14. Hungary / 13%
15. Netherlands / 12%
16. Spain / 12%

17. United States / 12%
18. Ireland / 12%
19. Bulgaria / 12%
20. Portugal / 12%

IMPLICATIONS OF THE AGE BOOM

Peter Peterson uses startling words in his book *Gray Dawn*: "There's an iceberg ahead. It's called global aging, and it threatens to bankrupt the great powers. . . . Now is the time to ring the alarm bell."[2]

Along with seniors living longer, there is a decrease in children being born. The birthrate of families today is approximately 26 percent less than the birthrate in 1970, and a whopping 75 percent less than in 1800. This combination of a low birthrate and extended years for seniors presents serious challenges for the future.

President Carter predicts a severe crunch in Social Security, Medicare, and Medicaid by 2013 unless "basic changes are made."[3] I believe these changes will be made; however, continued thought and action must be brought to bear on these issues now.

When Social Security began in the United States in 1935, approximately forty wage earners supported one retiree. By 1990, there were only 3.3 wage earners for each retiree. It has been predicted that by 2010 there will be only two workers paying for each retiree. Health care faces similar difficulties, and changes must be made for the sake of our children and grandchildren. Seniors are growing in number and using more of America's health care dollars.

The question is, Will the seniors of America and the world use their know-how, money, maturity, and political might to face and resolve these problems? I pray they will. The American Association of Retired People (AARP) boasts that it speaks for over thirty million seniors. Obviously, the potential of seniors for good is awesome and urgent.

OBSTACLES AND OPPORTUNITIES

Along with the alarm bell of obstacles comes the welcome bell of opportunity calling seniors to become aware of all they can *be* and *do.*

A reservoir of talent is waiting to be enlisted. Volunteerism is not dead. It's alive in our towns, cities, and churches, waiting to be mobilized for our children and grandchildren.

Specifically, seniors have *time to give.* Eighty-five percent of seniors are reasonably healthy and able to serve. (Fewer than 5 percent of seniors live in nursing homes.) They represent a huge reservoir of time, while they themselves have a need for daily meaning and fulfillment. Seniors are also the memory of the past. They help keep history alive, connecting how things *were* with how things *are.*

Many seniors have *money to give.* Because their basic lifetime needs have been met, they are able and willing to give to causes they sincerely believe in.

Seniors have *skills to pass on.* They exemplify how to survive. They can share the dangers as well as possibilities of life. They can be teachers and role models. "Consider the years of many generations. Ask your father, and he will show you; your elders, and they will tell you" (Deuteronomy 32:7). Seniors can show and tell and be a light in the darkness. Seniors can be the historians and storytellers in the community.

Each year I visit dozens of faith-based organizations. Many are managed by talented seniors. Scores thrive with the use of senior volunteers. In fact, some organizations couldn't exist without seniors. There is an ocean of untapped seniors in our churches and society waiting to be enlisted.

The age boom is an enormous open door for seniors to serve.

JOHN ANDERSON MY JO

John Anderson my jo, John, When we were first acquent;
Your locks were like the raven. Your bony brow was brent;

But now your brow is beld, John, Your locks are like the snow;
But blessings on your frosty pow, John Anderson my jo.

John Anderson my jo, John, We clamb the hill the gither;
And monie a canty day, John, We've had wi' ane anither;

Now we maun totter down, John, And hand in hand we'll go;
And sleep the gither at the foot, John Anderson my jo.

—Robert Burns

For age is opportunity no less
Than youth itself, though in another dress;
And as evening twilight fades away
The sky is filled with stars invisible by day.

—HENRY WADSWORTH LONGFELLOW
(Written for his fiftieth anniversary
upon graduating from Boudoin College)

⸺⸻⸺

Joys are always on the way to us.
They are always traveling to us through
the darkness of the night.
There is never a night when they are not coming.

—AMY CARMICHAEL

⸺⸻⸺

Joy is not gush; joy is not jolliness. Joy is perfect
acquiescence in
God's will because the soul delights itself in God Himself.

—H. W. WEBB-PEPLOE

⸺⸻⸺

Old age has its pleasures, which though different,
are no less than the pleasures of youth.

—W. SOMERSET MAUGHAM

⸺⸻⸺

Enjoy the little things . . . for one day you may look
back and realize . . . they were the big things.

—ROBERT BRAULT

The hard fact is that aging will bring unpleasant changes, among them, aches and pains; decreased vigor, healing ability, sensory acuity, muscle tone, bone density, and sexual energy; memory deficits; wrinkles; loss of beauty, friends, family, and independence; increased reliance on doctors and pills; and social isolation. We can mask the outward signs of the process or try to keep up old routines in spite of it, but we cannot change the fact that we are all moving toward physical decline and death. The best we can do—and it is a lot—is to accept this inevitability and try to adapt to it, to be in the best health we can at any age.

—ANDREW WEIL, M.D.

Even youths grow tired and weary,
and young men stumble and fall; but those who
hope in the Lord will renew their strength.
They will soar on wings like eagles;
they will run and not grow weary,
they will walk and not be faint.

—ISAIAH 40:30–31 (NIV)

Chapter 5

AGING
WITH JOY

O ne of the famous riddles of ancient literature is the "Riddle of the Sphinx": "What goes on four feet, then two feet, and then on three, but the more feet it goes on, the weaker it be?" The answer is man! In childhood, he creeps on all fours. As an adult, he walks erect on two feet. In old age, he is weak and steadies himself with a cane.

All of life is a journey. We move from the helplessness of childhood to the strength of adults, and if life lasts long enough, we return to weakness and dependence again. However, it is possible to *age with joy*, and that's the theme of this chapter.

Joy does not mean the absence of pain or freedom from the normal effects of aging. Rather, joy is an attitude that grows out of trust . . . that God is in charge.

The Random House Unabridged Dictionary defines joy as "an emotion of great delight caused by something good or satisfying." Synonyms listed are bliss, rapture, delight, gladness, and rejoicing. However, Christian joy includes infinitely more.

Joy, according to Paul the apostle, is the fruit of God the Holy Spirit guiding our lives (Galatians 5:22). Joy is a by-product of knowing God, resulting in a confidence that God is fully in charge of all of life . . . come what may!

Of course, most of us agree that old age comes too fast. As my German father-in-law used to say, "Too soon old, too late smart." Frankly, I'm shocked at the brevity of life.

In *To the Good Long Life*, Morton Puner quotes the British writer J. B. Priestly. When asked, at age seventy-nine, what it's like to be old, Priestly answered, "It's as though I was walking down Shaftsburg Avenue as a fairly young man, and I was suddenly kidnapped, rushed into a theater and made to don the gray hair, the wrinkles and other marks of age—then wheeled on stage. Yet behind the appearance of age, I'm still the very same person with the same thoughts as when I was younger."[1]

At age eighty-three, I agree with J. B. Priestly. As a young man I had dark-brown curly hair, but now it's white and wavy . . . and it's waving bye-bye. However, I still think like I did in my forties. I also plan like I did in my forties and then panic . . . when I can't do what my mind has planned.

CHALLENGE AND CHANGE

Aging forces change. The later years are times when most people cut back from earlier occupations to allow for more leisure and personal pursuits. Younger minds and hands take up the tasks that once were ours.

As we age, we're forced to find new roles to fill. I have found enjoyment in helping others prepare to take over and have reveled in their success. As we age, we discover slowly but surely that our strength and energy decrease. Often we experience a reluctance to act decisively; although we are present and involved, a detachment gradually begins to evolve.

Society and science historically have promoted a negative

view of aging. William Shakespeare showed his bias when he
wrote,

Crabbed age and youth cannot live together:
Youth is full of pleasance, age is full of care;
Youth, like summer morn, age like winter weather;
Youth, like summer brave, age like winter bare.
Youth is full of sport, age's breath is short;
Youth is nimble, age is lame; Youth is hot and bold, age
   is weak and cold;
Youth is wild, and age is tame;
Age, I do abhor thee, youth I do adore thee.

—FROM "THE PASSIONATE PILGRIM," 1590

Continually, we're bombarded with images and words
shouting, Youth is beautiful and old age is a disaster! I agree
that youth is beautiful, but I believe old age is equally beautiful. Age adds maturity and richness to life. Age replaces shal-
lowness with depth. Age smoothes the rough edges of life and
adds gentleness and compassion. They say, "The older the violin, the sweeter the music!" Some speak of seniors as ancient,
faded, frail, shriveled, senile, withered, wrinkled, and worth-
less! I like to use other words like experienced, dependable,
mature, patient, seasoned, steady, wise, tested, survivor . . .
veterans!

At first glance, even the Bible seems to suggest that the clos-
ing years of life are tough. "Remember now your Creator in the
days of your youth, before *the difficult days come,* and the years
draw near when you say, 'I have no pleasure in them'" (Ecclesiastes 12:1, italics added). That's a depressing picture painted
by Solomon. One translation calls these last days of life "evil
days" (NASB).

Solomon adds details that are the pits. He describes the
bodily decay of growing older. The "keepers of the house" (the

arms and hands) begin to tremble. The "strong men" (limbs and feet) will "bow down" as they grow more feeble. The "grinders" (teeth) will "cease because they are few." The passage goes on to say, "And those that look through the windows" (eyes) will be dimmed by advancing years. And the inescapable end . . . is death (Ecclesiastes 12:3–4).

I smiled as I read some imagined advantages to aging.

1. Most of life's struggles are past.
2. Your secrets are safe with your friends . . . because they can't remember them either.
3. There's very little left to learn . . . the hard way.
4. Kidnappers are not interested in you.
5. You can have a big party, and the neighbors don't even realize it.
6. You can get into a heated argument over pension plans.
7. You can eat dinner at 4:30 p.m.
8. You quit trying to hold your stomach in.
9. Your investment into health insurance is finally paying off.
10. Your joints are more accurate than the weather service.

However, more seriously for those of faith, age has a richness of experience, a certain serenity, grace—and also, joy.

ACCEPTANCE

Everything in the universe ages. To deny aging is to hinder or miss the many positive opportunities that aging offers. Acceptance is crucial to success and enjoyment.

One of the joys of aging is more leisure time. We find release from the obligations of daily work. I enjoy listening to the morning traffic report while occasionally catching a few more winks. Though retirement offers unique opportunities, we need to ward off a retirement mentality. I prefer to think of the senior years as a time of special service. Former President Jimmy Carter and his wife, Rosalyn, are choice role models as they are actively involved in major and minor ways to help people. At times, this includes serving abroad or working with Habitat for Humanity constructing homes for the needy or doing service in their local church.

Don and Naomi Cole, though in their mideighties, have returned several times to Angola, Africa, to share with families and churches they served thirty years earlier as missionaries. Retirement is a marvelous chance to match your talents with your passions . . . in service to others.

My personal part-time retirement has been so gradual as to be almost painless, allowing me to pursue my passions, only at my own pace. So far, I have found that I can do most things nearly as well as before, only for a shorter duration of time. To suddenly retire with no plans for a meaningful use of time can be devastating. Retirement should be wisely planned.

Another great joy is to enter into the lives of our children, grandchildren, and great-grandchildren, and I can verify that there is no joy quite like watching them grow. I'm a happy member of the SOGPIP (Silly Old Grandparents Pictures in Pocket).

We do our best to celebrate each of their birthdays with a phone call followed by breakfast or lunch at a convenient time. Since four grandchildren live a thousand miles away, we schedule their birthday event when we visit. We have rarely missed celebrating with each grandchild, and our oldest is now in his thirties.

We have several picnics a year with twenty to thirty others, and the grandchildren rarely miss. Each grandchild has a key to our home, and knows, come what may, we are there for them.

POSITIVE OPPORTUNITIES OF AGING

Our senior years should also be a time of significant *growth.* Anyone who stops growing is old whether he's nineteen or ninety. The apostle Paul was told that suffering was to be part of his future, yet as he says farewell to the elders of the church of Ephesus, he tells them: "None of these things move me; nor do I count my life dear to myself, so that I may finish my race *with joy"* (Acts 20:24, italics added). It is possible to age . . . with joy.

Because aging reminds us of dying, it can be a major wake-up call to spiritual change and growth. I like to remember that when Paul made this statement he had no idea what was in his future. Yet he was willing to give God a blank check and let Him fill it in. He was a growing person.

Each of us is invited to do the same with our senior years. We can say, I want to finish my life *with joy.*

Retirement offers the chance to refine our character. Like the burning bush that drew Moses in the wilderness, God may want to make your life a bright light to glow in the darkness that will in turn encourage others along the way.

Psalm 71 is called the psalm for seniors. The psalmist voices some of the feelings that accompany aging but also states his strong desire to be *a light* in the darkness: "Since my youth . . . you have taught me, and to this day I declare your marvelous deeds. Even when I am old and gray, do not forsake me, O God, *till I declare your power* to the next generation, your might to all who are to come" (verses 17–18 NIV, italics added).

Each senior has the privilege—and I might add the responsibility—of sharing God's ways with the next generation. Our senior years need not be pointless, but rather useful, as we pass the torch to others. Like Caleb we say "Give me this mountain" as a legacy to our grandchildren and great-grandchildren.

BUILDING THE INNER LIFE

Early in life, I came to the conclusion that the inner life was of lasting importance. During my college days, I asked questions like, "Why am I here? What is my reason for existing?" Slowly but surely, I realized my outer life was temporal, fragile, and transitory. By contrast, the inner life, though unseen, offered enormous possibilities. The physical life inevitably declines—whereas the inner life can grow stronger.

Retirement offers a unique opportunity to focus on the inside. The apostle Paul put it this way: "We do not lose heart. Even though our outward man is perishing, yet the *inward man* is being renewed day by day" (2 Corinthians 4:16, italics added). Aging reminds us of our mortality and is a stimulus to spiritual growth.

Many years ago while vacationing on the New Jersey ocean shore, I read an unforgettable sentence from Anne Morrow Lindbergh's book, *Gift from the Sea*. She writes, "Simplification of the outward life is not enough. It is merely the outside. But I am starting with the outside. I am looking at the outside of a shell, the outside of my life—the shell. The complete answer is not to be found on the outside, in an outward mode of living. This is only a technique, a road to grace. The final answer, I know, is always inside."[2]

"The final answer . . . is always inside." Regardless of age, there are things we can do *right now* to change the inside.

First, we need to be convinced that there is an inner life . . . and it needs to be nurtured. Despite the hectic demands of daily life, only that which is eternal ultimately matters. In my first year of college, I read *Practicing the Presence of God* by Brother Lawrence. I resolved to consciously seek God's presence in the ordinary deeds of everyday living.

Aging is an invitation to focus on the inside. Blaise Pascal said, "All men's miseries derive from not being able to sit quietly in a room *alone.*" Rather than being discouraged because of physical decline, we can focus on "the inside."

Second, I made a conscious effort to pursue the reading of great books. Nothing refreshes me like a book. Through reading, we can travel the world and listen to the brightest and the best. Through reading, pain will lessen, and we're able to rise above the nagging irritations of daily situations. I cannot overemphasize the importance of feeding and stimulating the mind and heart. A sincere thirst to grow is a vital ingredient to aging with joy.

For me, several chapters of the Bible a day lift my spirit and ignite my soul. This, coupled with quietness, study, and prayer, is life building. My goal is to renew "the inside."

Third, I faithfully pursue corporate as well as individual worship, to encourage "the inside." Worship is the communion of our souls with God. It means rubbing our cold lives against the beauty of His holiness. Scripture reminds us *not* to forsake "the assembling of ourselves together" (Hebrews 10:25). Corporate worship renews "the inside."

However, corporate worship must be undergirded by individual worship. Sometimes we refer to this as *devotions* or *quiet time.* Whatever the name, it's that time each day when we give ourselves to God—to reacknowledge His lordship.

The Psalms have been life-giving to me. During two surgeries, I peacefully went into surgery quoting, "The Lord is the strength of my life; of whom shall I be afraid?" (Psalm 27:1).

Several years ago, while vacationing at the ocean, I walked the sandy beach with my four-year-old granddaughter Katie. After walking a considerable distance, she tired and asked me to carry her. However, I too was struggling with the soft sand and the slope of the beach and told my granddaughter I was unable to carry her. She looked up at me, as only a four-year-old granddaughter can do, and said, "Grandpa, if you carry me *now* . . . when you're old and little, I'll carry you." Wow!

Whereupon, I experienced an infusion of supernatural strength, swept her into my arms, and carried her all the way home with little effort and great joy.

Upon arriving at our apartment, I shared this experience with my wife. She exclaimed, "That's Isaiah 46:4: 'Even to your old age and gray hairs I am he, I am he who will sustain you. I have made you and will *carry you*'" (NIV, italics added). Both of us read that verse several times and claimed it for our senior years.

Little Katie is now a lovely twenty-year-old young lady. Last Easter, following Sunday dinner, I teasingly asked Katie if she was now strong enough to carry me. She answered, "Grandpa, I thought you would shrink as you grew older, but the way you look . . . I'll never be able to carry you!" Katie then added, "Grandpa, though I can't carry you in my arms, I'll always carry you in my heart." Yes, yes, . . . we can age with joy!

A SEVENTEENTH-CENTURY NUN'S PRAYER

Lord, Thou knowest better than myself
Know that I am growing older and will someday be old.
Keep me from the fatal habit of thinking I must say
something on every subject and on every occasion.
Release me from the craving to
straighten out everybody's affairs.
Make me thoughtful, but not moody; helpful, but not bossy.
With my vast store of wisdom it seems a pity not to use it all,
But Thou knowest, O Lord, that I want a few friends at the end.
Keep my mind free from the recital of endless details;
Give me wings to get to the point,
Seal my lips on my aches and pains,
They are increasing, and love of rehearsing them
is becoming sweeter as the days go by.
I dare not ask for grace enough to
enjoy the tales of others' pains,
But help me to endure them with patience.
I dare not ask for an improved memory,
But for a growing humility and a lessening cocksureness
when my memory seems to clash
with the memories of others.
Teach me the glorious lesson that occasionally I may be
mistaken. Keep me reasonably sweet;
I do not want to be a saint; Some
of them are so hard to live with—
But a sour old person is one of the
crowning works of the devil.
Give me the ability to see good things in unexpected places,
and talents in unexpected people. And give me,
O Lord, the grace to tell them so.
Amen.

Because you have an occasional spell of despondency,
do not despair. After all, remember that the sun has a sinking
spell every night but rises again in the morning.

—UNKNOWN

Optimism can be learned. And optimists do better than
pessimists in almost every aspect of life, including
how well their immune systems function.

—ANDREW WEIL, M.D.

I married an archaeologist because the older
I grow, the more he appreciates me.

—AGATHA CHRISTIE

And so, generally speaking, old people seem to be divided into
two well-defined categories with few intermediate shades.
There are the wonderful old people, kind, sociable, radiant with
peace. Trouble and difficulties only seem to make them grow
still further in serenity. They make no claims, and it is a
pleasure to see them and to help them. They are grateful, and
even astonished, that things are done for them, and that they
are still loved. They read, they improve their minds, they go for
quiet walks, they are interested in everything and are prepared
to listen to anyone. And then there are awful old people,
selfish, demanding, domineering, bitter. They are always
grumbling and criticizing everybody. If you go and see them,
they upbraid you for not having come sooner; they misjudge
your best intentions, and the conversation becomes a painful
conflict.

—PAUL TOURNIER

Chapter 6

ARTERIES
PLUS
ATTITUDE

Recently I read a book that included a chapter titled, "Attitudes, Not Arteries." The author was helpful generally; however, the title suggested a person's arteries are unimportant. Nothing could be further from the truth. If your arteries are clogged, regardless of your attitude, you will probably die!

After consulting with several doctors, I am convinced that nothing keeps a person healthier than keeping the cardiovascular system healthy. Research affirms that more people die from cardiovascular disease than from any other cause. Michael F. Roizen, M.D., reminds us in his book *Real Age* that our "arteries are like streets that eventually wear out. They become blocked with a substance called plaque. As the arteries grow older and clogged they are subject to clots."[1]

What can we do to prevent arterial aging? We can eat right. A diet low in saturated fat is the place to begin. Exercise and the ability to avoid stress are two ways to improve arterial health. Careless living and inactivity ages the cardiovascular system more quickly. Poor food choices result in added weight, and added weight hinders exercise. Arterial health is something to strive after.

Though the emphasis of this chapter concerns a person's attitude, always remember that healthy arteries are vital to successful aging.

ATTITUDES ARE IMPORTANT ALSO

Because each person is unique, attitudes vary greatly. Some face aging pessimistically and appear to increase the difficulties of life while others take a more positive view.

Victor S. Frankl tells of his experiences in a concentration camp during World War II: "We who lived in the concentration camps can remember the men who walked through the huts comforting others, giving away their last piece of bread. They may have been few in number, but they offer sufficient proof that everything can be taken from a man but one thing, the last of his freedoms—to choose one's attitudes in any given set of circumstances, to choose one's own way."

To choose your attitude toward aging is a mind-stretching challenge and just might be life extending. I heard Clement Stone say, "There is little difference in people, but that little difference makes a big difference. That little difference is attitude."

Experts in aging make a distinction between passive aging and purposeful aging. Successful, purposeful aging calls for continued involvement, relationships, discipline, and an attitude of faith.

Three old-timers were playing a round of golf. One complained about the oppressive humidity. The other griped about the roughness of the greens. The third was more optimistic and quipped, "At least we're on the right side of the grass."

Michael DeSaint-Pierre comments, "An optimist may see a light where there is none, but why must the pessimist always run to blow it out? It's been said that when pessimists meet, they don't shake hands . . . they shake heads."

A story is told of a duck hunter and his sensational dog. Whenever he shot a flying duck, his dog would run *on top of the water* and retrieve the duck. However, his hunting buddies never appeared to notice or comment about this extraordinary dog. On one occasion, after downing several ducks, he could no longer stand their silence and asked directly, "Didn't you notice anything unusual about my hunting dog?" To which they responded, "Yes, he can't swim!"

IT'S NATURAL TO BE NEGATIVE

It's natural to be negative in life. Contrary to the views of some, there is a place for negative thinking. Some things are always wrong and must be recognized as harmful. For example, the Ten Commandments call attention to several negative acts: "You shall *not* murder. You shall *not* commit adultery. You shall *not* steal" (Exodus 20:13–15, italics added).

The apostle Paul wrote that creation groans because of the fall of man (Romans 8:22). The voice of nature, whether it's the wind, waves, beasts of the field, or birds of the air, is heard in the minor key. All of creation groans. Paul goes on to say, "*We also* who have the firstfruits of the Spirit . . . groan within ourselves . . . waiting for . . . the redemption of our body" (Romans 8:23, italics added). Groaning is normal, and even natural for all people, including those who are people of great faith.

I must confess that occasionally I groan while on my daily walks. When my wife chides me for groaning, I remind her with a smile that "groaning is biblical." However, Paul speaks of a day when our natures will be changed from discord to harmony and from imperfection to perfection. Then we will have ageless bodies, and we will groan no more.

Paul continues to tell how we can cultivate an attitude of joy . . . *now*, in this life, if we choose.

AN ATTITUDE OF JOY

While in a Roman jail, Paul illustrates an attitude of joy. He said, "The things which happened to me have actually turned out for the furtherance of the gospel" (Philippians 1:12).

Conceivably, Paul could have groaned about his imprisonment and written:

Dear Friends,
I have discovered that it really doesn't pay to serve God. Notice where I am: in jail, and I don't like it one bit. To think I've been faithful all these years, and I end up in prison. I'm disappointed, bitter, and resentful.
                    Unhappily yours, the apostle Paul

By contrast, consider this expanded paraphrase (Philippians 1:12–14):

Dear Friends,
I want you to know this is the first time I've ever had a mission tour paid for by the Roman government. But more than that, they chain soldiers to me for twenty-four hours a day; and I share with them. Every eight hours, they change the guards, and I have a new congregation. Some are coming to faith in Caesar's palace. I'm having a ball. Wish you were here. Keep up the support.
                    Joyfully yours, the apostle Paul

Possibly, you're thinking, *How can I build a joyful, believing attitude in a negative world?* Paul suggests two ways. "If God is for us, who can be against us?" (Romans 8:31). This could be paraphrased, "Since God is for us, it doesn't really matter who's against us." He reminds his audience that God is not neutral about His own but is enthusiastically *for us*. That's mind stretching.

There are times in life when we're not even for ourselves, yet God *is for* us, *with* us, *helping* us, and *cheering* us on. The knowledge that God is actively for us is good news in a challenging world.

The following verse offers an even greater promise, assuring us that "He who did not spare His own Son, but delivered Him up for us all, how shall He not with Him *also freely give us all things!*" (Romans 8:32, italics added). The gift of God's Son is infinite and beyond imagination and yet, in addition to this, God promises every conceivable thing *we need to survive and thrive!*

AN ATTITUDE OF THANKS

I'm invited, by prayer and supplication, with thanksgiving, to let my requests be made known to God (Philippians 4:6).

It's easy to be thankful when life flows along like a song—when the sky is blue, the sun shines brightly, and the gentle breezes blow. But what about those times when health wanes and money is scarce? Can we be thankful then?

The psalmist wrote, "Many . . . are Your wonderful works . . . and Your thoughts toward us . . . they are more than can be numbered" (Psalm 40:5).

The power of a grateful spirit is hard to exaggerate. An attitude of thankfulness encourages a feeling of well-being. Occasionally, I list a few of the things for which I'm thankful. For example:

1. Faith in a caring heavenly Father
2. The love of family and friends
3. Health that is reasonably good
4. The challenge and enjoyment of work
5. The privilege of contributing to the lives of others
6. The ability to meet my financial obligations

7. A good night's sleep
8. Waking up to the smell of coffee and burnt toast (I like burnt toast.)
9. More than my daily bread to eat
10. A daily walk with my wife and a little more coffee
11. The privilege of taking our grandchildren out to breakfast one at a time, and learning their likes and dislikes
12. Fellowship and inspiration with the people of our local church
13. Finding a parking place, especially when I'm late
14. Laughing enthusiastically until it hurts
15. An occasional afternoon nap—"nature's sweet restorative"
16. Pruning roses in our garden or picking berries
17. Reading a good book
18. Listening to old songs and remembering when . . .
19. Watching the sun rise and set
20. The sound of rain beating on the windowpane
21. Chatting with neighbors about small things

Especially, I'm thankful for the privilege *of prayer.* That in all the experiences of my life, I'm invited "by prayer and supplication, with *thanksgiving,* [to] let [my] requests be made known to God" (Philippians 4:6, italics added).

The worst moment for an atheist must be when he's really thankful and has no one to thank.

Clean arteries plus an attitude of joy and thanks are important to successful aging, and each . . . involves a conscious choice.

THANKS IN OLD AGE

Thanks in old age—thanks ere I go.
For health, the midday sun, the
impalpable air—for life, mere life.
For precious ever-lingering memories,
(of you my mother dear—you, father—
you, brothers, sisters, friends,)
For all my days—not those of peace alone—
days of war the same,
For gentle words, caresses, gifts from foreign lands,
For shelter, wine and meat—for sweet appreciation,
(You distant, dim unknown—or young or old—
countless, unspecified, readers belov'd,
We never met, and ne'er shall meet—
and yet our souls embrace, long, close and long;)
For beings, groups, love, deeds, words,
books—for colors, forms,
For all the brave strong men—devoted, hardy men—
who've forward sprung in freedom's help, all years, all lands,
For braver, stronger, more devoted men—
(a special laurel ere I go, to life's war's chosen ones,
The cannoneers of song and thought—the great
artillerists—the foremost leaders, captains of the soul:)
As soldier from an ended war return'd—
as traveler out of myriads, to the
long procession retrospective,
Thanks—joyful thanks!—a soldier's, traveler's thanks.

—WALT WHITMAN (1819–1892)

We have a lot of evidence that shows mirth and laughter
affect most of the major physical systems of the body.

—Dr. William F. Fry Jr.

⸻

Ten minutes of genuine belly laughter had an anesthetic effect
and would give me at least two hours of pain-free sleep.

—Norman Cousins

⸻

I have seen what a laugh can do. It can transform almost
unbearable tears into something bearable—even hopeful.

—Comedian Bob Hope

⸻

Laughter is a form of internal jogging.

—Norman Cousins

⸻

If I can make people smile, then
I have served my purpose for God.

—Comedian Red Skelton

⸻

You can turn painful situations around through laughter.
If you can find humor in anything—
even in poverty—you can survive it.

—Comedian Bill Cosby

It is bad to suppress laughter.
It goes back down and spreads to your hips.

—COMEDIAN FRED ALLEN

———

Humor opposes directly those emotions which have been specifically recorded as being associated with precipitation of heart attack. These emotions are fear and rage. Humor acts to relieve fear. Rage is impossible when mirth prevails.

—DR. WILLIAM F. FRY JR.

———

It is pleasing to the dear God whenever thou rejoicest or laughest from the bottom of thy heart.

—MARTIN LUTHER

———

Like a welcome summer rain, humor may suddenly cleanse and cool the earth, the air, and you.

—LANGSTON HUGHES

———

If you wish to glimpse inside a human soul and get to know a man, don't bother analyzing his ways of being silent, of talking, of weeping, of seeing how much he is moved by noble ideas; you will get better results if you just watch him laugh. If he laughs well, he's a good man.

—FYODOR DOSTOEVSKY

Old age is when you get out of the shower
and you're glad the mirror is all fogged up.

* * * *

The seven ages of man: spills,
drills, thrills, bills, ills, pills, wills.

—RICHARD NEEDHAM

———

There are four stages to life—
1. As a child you believe in Santa Claus.
2. Then you don't believe in Santa Claus.
3. As you age, you look like Santa Claus.
4. Finally, you think you are Santa Claus.

—ANONYMOUS

———

Being 80 is a lot better than being 70. At 70, people
are mad at you for everything. At 80, you have a perfect
excuse no matter what you do. If you act foolishly,
it's your second childhood. Everybody is looking for
symptoms of softening of the brain.

—FRANK C. LAUBACH

———

Old age: When actions creak louder than words.

—DANA ROBBINS

———

A person without a sense of humor
is like a wagon without springs—
jolted by every pebble in the road.

—HENRY WARD BEECHER

Chapter 7

WHY COMEDIANS LIVE SO LONG

B efore this chapter is finished, I believe you will have the answer to the question, "Why do comedians live so long?" Of course, I can't prove it, but there appears to be a positive relationship between humor and longevity. At least a sense of humor helps to cope with the stresses of life and just might have life-extending value. Comedians give their lives to help people laugh and, in return, appear to benefit by extra years.

LAUGHTER REDUCES STRESS

George Vaillant, in his studies of a large group of male Harvard graduates, "consistently found that a sense of humor is associated not only with good physical health, but also with superior psychological adjustment." Vaillant considers humor to be the best coping mechanism available to us. He goes on to say, "We use humor both to recognize hard realities and protect ourselves from their inherent sorrow and hurt."[1]

Laughter has been called "the safety valve of the nervous system," and I might add, so are tears. However, tears are draining and sloppy. Laughter relaxes the body much like ordinary exercise.

William Fry, a researcher from Stanford University, believes that laughter increases disease-fighting antibodies into the bloodstream, enabling the body to ward off infection.

Decades ago, Jonathan Swift wrote, "The best doctors in the world are Dr. Diet, Dr. Quiet, and Dr. Merryman." The word *merry* means full of laughter, lively, cheerful. Thousands of years ago, Solomon wrote, "Pleasant words are like a honeycomb, sweetness to the soul and health to the bones" (Proverbs 16:24). Are pleasant words sweet? Can laughter bring health to our bones? Solomon also said, "A merry heart makes a cheerful countenance, but by sorrow of the heart the spirit is broken" (Proverbs 15:13). There's no doubt about it: Cheerful people look better!

While I was recovering from prostate surgery, a friend sent me a card with this verse: "A merry heart does good, like medicine, but a broken spirit dries the bones" (Proverbs 17:22). Is laughter good, like medicine? Is a gloomy spirit life draining? My surgeon felt the answer was yes, in both cases.

In most books on aging, humor is high on the list of things that contribute to a sense of enjoyment and longevity. So learn to laugh . . . it's good for you.

LAUGHTER IS THERAPEUTIC

Executive Digest magazine states:

Scientists have been studying the effects of laughter on human beings and have found that laughter has a profound and instantaneous effect on virtually every important organ in the human body. Laughter reduces health-sapping tensions and relaxes the tissues as well as exercising the most vital organs. It is said that laughter, even when forced, results in beneficial effects mentally and physically. Next time you feel nervous and jittery, *indulge in a good laugh.*[2]

Occasionally, someone will tell me he has nothing in life to laugh about. I urge him to try to laugh anyway. Even forced laughter can be helpful. Laughter *is* good medicine.

I recall a service in one of my pastorates when the choirmaster introduced the handbell choir. Inadvertently, he said, "And now . . . the *Handball* Choir." We enjoyed a good laugh.

On another occasion, the church sanctuary was filled with four thousand people waiting for a concert to begin. The program was to be broadcast. When it was time to begin, the engineer from the sound room pointed to the conductor to begin, but the conductor didn't respond. Unaware that the microphone was open, the engineer blurted out for all to hear, like a voice from heaven, "Tell the old goat to get the show on the road." A startled audience broke into laughter.

Laughter is good medicine (Proverbs 17:22). Laughter is exercise. Can you ever remember laughing 'til it hurt? . . . 'til you became light-headed?

Norman Cousins, onetime editor of *The Saturday Review*, was told at age thirty-nine that he had three months to live. After reading about the relationship of stress to health, he determined to pursue laughter as a stress reducer. He began a daily routine of watching humorous films or TV programs like *Candid Camera*, Abbot and Costello, *I Love Lucy*, and *The Honeymooners*. He read upbeat stories and literature of a humorous, uplifting nature.

Not only did he find relief from pain, but he lived an additional thirty-nine years (dying in 1990 at age seventy-eight). He also became adjunct professor in the Department of Behavioral Medicine at the University of California, Los Angeles, School of Medicine.

Pleasant words do, indeed, appear to be health building. Laughter is the best medicine available, and it's hard to overdose!

DOES GOD HAVE A SENSE OF HUMOR?

Of all the creatures created by God, only man has the ability to laugh. Recently, I was asked at a seminar if God had a sense of humor.

Ecclesiastes 3:4 tells us there is "a time to laugh." The psalmist also speaks of God laughing at the presumption of rebellious people (Psalm 2:4). Because all people are made in God's likeness—and we have a sense of humor—it seems logical that God has a sense of humor too.

When Abraham at age one hundred and his wife, Sarah, at age ninety were told they would have a son, Sarah said, "God has made me laugh, and all who hear will laugh with me" (Genesis 21:6). They named their miracle baby *Isaac*, which means "to laugh."

Occasionally, I have smiled while reading Paul's letter to Timothy: "Alexander the coppersmith did me much harm. May the Lord repay him according to his works" (2 Timothy 4:14).

Abraham Lincoln said, "God must have meant us to laugh, else He would not have made so many mules, parrots, monkeys . . . and human beings."

The older I get, the more I enjoy people-watching—it's hilarious! And I know that people are laughing at me as well.

Helen Salsbury wrote,

> *Dear God, we make You so solemn,*
> *So stiff and staid—*
> *How can we be so foolish*
> *When we look at the things You've made?*
> *How can we miss the twinkle,*
> *That must have been in Your eye,*

When You planned the hippopotami
And the rhinoceri?
Who watches an ostrich swallow,
Then doubts that You like to play,
Or questions Your sense of humor,
Hearing a donkey bray?
Could the God who made the monkey
Have forgotten how to laugh—
Or the One who striped the zebra
And stretched out the giraffe?
How could a solemn God
Fashion a pelican—
Or a perfectly somber Creator
Ever imagine man?[2]

Someone may respond that someday we will give account for idle words (Matthew 12:36). Les Flynn writes, "Humorous words are not necessarily idle words, any more than some serious words. Idle words are those *without a purpose.* Since the purpose of words is to carry on the business of life, encourage others, and refresh the mind, any word designed to bring relief from the . . . monotonous pressures of life is not idle."[3]

Faith does not oppose humor, rather it opposes the abuse of humor. Humor is part of life. Humor that is hurtful or sordid is offensive and dangerous, but good humor is a special gift from God.

Les Flynn writes, "Laughing can be as spiritual as singing or crying. A moderate . . . use of our sense of humor is not incompatible with joy."[4]

A reporter interviewed a man on his 100th birthday. "Tell me, sir, to what do you attribute your longevity?" The oldster replied, "To the fact that I was born . . . a long, long time ago."

"To what do you attribute your long life?" the reporter asked a man who was celebrating his 107th birthday. "Don't know for sure yet," said the old-timer. "My lawyer's negotiating with two breakfast-food companies."

On one of his rare trips to the city, Grandpa was so fascinated by a large building's elevator that he stood in front of one for several minutes. He watched an old lady, bent and wrinkled, enter. He saw the door close and she was gone. Moments later, he watched amazed as the same door opened and out stepped an attractive young lady. Grandpa pushed for the door, shouting, "I'm gonna bring Grandma here!"

A reporter was interviewing three wrinkle-faced codgers on a park bench. He asked the first, "What do you do for amusement, and how old are you?" He answered, "I play checkers, and I am ninety-eight." To the same question, the second old man replied, "I play chess, and I am ninety-five." And the third replied, "I drink alcohol every day, smoke ten cigars, and stay up all night." "Your age?" the reporter asked. "Twenty-nine."

The reporter interviewed a woman who was celebrating her 100th birthday. "How do you do it?" he asked. "Well," she said, "I never rocked any of our twelve children to sleep. I never got up with them nights. I never washed dishes or cleaned the house. My dear husband, Henry, did that. May he rest in peace; he died at forty-nine."

From a lifetime of much joy and also sorrow, I can attest to the truth of Proverbs 16:24: "Pleasant words are like a honeycomb, sweetness to the soul and *health to the bones*" (italics added). Those who laugh . . . last!

Every life is a profession of faith, and exercises an inevitable and silent propaganda. As far as lies in its power, it tends to transform the universe and humanity into its own image. Thus we have all a cure of souls. Every man is a centre of perpetual radiation like a luminous body; he is, as it were, a beacon which entices a ship upon the rocks if it does not guide it into port. Every man is a priest, even involuntarily; his conduct is an unspoken sermon, which is forever preaching to others, . . . Such is the high importance of example.

—HENRI FREDERIC AMIEL

A man who lives right, and is right, has more power
in his silence than another has by his words.

—PHILLIPS BROOKS

He that gives good advice builds with one hand; he that gives good counsel and example builds with both; but he that gives good admonition and bad example builds with one hand and pulls down with the other.

—FRANCIS BACON

It is easier to exemplify values than teach them.

—THEODORE HESBURGH

Follow my example, as I follow the example of Christ.

—THE APOSTLE PAUL, 1 Corinthians 11:1 (NIV)

Come, follow me . . . and I will make you fishers of men.

—JESUS, Matthew 4:19 (NIV)

Chapter 8

ROLE
MODELS
FOR AGING

T he pastor of my childhood church served the same congregation for over sixty-two years. When I asked him why
he never left in all those years, he modestly replied, "No one
ever asked me to leave." Honest humility was a character trait
that made him so attractive.

He was such a mega influence on my formative years that
he became my lifetime role model. His example was so com-
pelling that following my college and seminary studies, I became his associate in my home church.

I never saw him lose his composure. To me he was the epit-
ome of patience, reliability, and compassion. During his lifetime he began and grew a wonderful church that continues to
this day.

I too have had the joy of serving in the ministry for over
sixty years as pastor of four churches and then president and
chancellor of a college for an additional twenty-nine years.
When I face major challenges, even to this day, I still find myself asking, How would my boyhood pastor solve this situation? He was to me a special role model. He also modeled aging
as he served full-time through his eighty-second year.

Jesus is the supreme role model for every earnest Christian. During His earthly life, He called twelve men to follow Him. On one occasion He saw Peter and Andrew casting their nets for fish. Calling them He said, "Come, follow me . . . and I will make you fishers of men" (Matthew 4:19 NIV). They left their nets and followed Him for the rest of their lives.

On another occasion, Paul the apostle used similar words. He urged the Christians in Corinth to "follow my example, as I follow the example of Christ" (1 Corinthians 11:1 NIV). Jesus is the supreme role model for all believers.

However, Jesus did not live a long earthly life. The gospel of Luke states that Jesus "was about thirty years old when he began his ministry" (Luke 3:23 NIV). Three years later He died at the hands of the Roman authorities. Jesus died in His prime and did not experience old age. His brief life is a powerful reminder that faithfulness to God's will is infinitely more important than longevity. Jesus exemplified submission to God's will even though it included crucifixion. Jesus' death clearly reminds us that obedience and submission are more important than clinging to life for personal advantage.

The New Testament says little about aging, probably because relatively few people lived to an advanced age. Tim Parkins, in his book *Roman Demography and Society*, tells us that "life expectancy at birth was about twenty-five years primarily because of the high infant mortality rate. Those over sixty years of age represented about 5 to 10 percent of the entire population."[1] However, we do find in the New Testament several role models who teach us about aging well.

NEW TESTAMENT ROLE MODELS

Zechariah and Elizabeth

The gospel of Luke introduces us to an attractive couple named Zechariah and Elizabeth. The Bible says that they were "well along in years." The King James Version reads, "both were now well stricken in years" (Luke 1:7).

They were also exemplary in every way, "upright in the sight of God . . . and blameless" (Luke 1:6 NIV). Both of them were descendents of a priestly family and served into their old age. The only negative was that Elizabeth was barren.

However, life changed radically for them when an angel visited Zechariah as he was serving the Lord in the temple. The angel told him his prayer had been heard and Elizabeth would give birth to a son in her old age. Zechariah asked, "How can I be sure of this? I am an old man and my wife is well along in years" (Luke 1:18 NIV). Zechariah was shocked and unbelieving! Because of this failure to believe, he was afflicted with the loss of speech. The narrative says, "When he came out, he could not speak to them" (Luke 1:22 NIV). Zechariah lost the ability to speak, during the entire pregnancy.

After the child was born, family and friends urged the couple to name the baby *Zechariah*, after his father. Both Elizabeth and Zechariah refused and called the baby John, according to the angel's instruction (Luke 1:13). Then Zechariah had his speech restored and he praised God (Luke 1:62–64).

Elizabeth and Zechariah were not only role models of exemplary living, but continued service into old age. These two seniors, along with Mary the mother of Jesus, were among the very first to announce God's salvation to the world.

Simeon and Anna

Luke also introduces us to Simeon and Anna, two remarkable seniors who individually served God in their later years.

Simeon had longed for the coming of the Messiah and had been promised to actually see Him before his death (Luke 2:26).

When Jesus was eight days old, Mary and Joseph brought Him to the temple and presented Him to the Lord. Immediately,

Simeon recognized the Christ-child as the long-awaited Messiah and broke into praise, saying:

> Sovereign Lord, as you have promised, you will dismiss your servant in peace. For my eyes have seen your salvation, which you have prepared in the sight of all people, a light for revelation to the Gentiles and for the glory of your people Israel. (Luke 2:29–32 NIV)

Anna, as a widow, also faithfully served in her senior years. Luke tells us, "she was very old"; at age eighty-four she "worshipped night and day fasting and praying" (Luke 2:36 NIV). Anna was a remarkable lady. When she met Mary, Joseph, and Jesus, "she gave thanks to God and spoke about the child to all who were looking forward to the redemption of Jerusalem" (Luke 2:38 NIV). She was an outspoken witness at age eighty-four.

Simeon and Anna are role models to all seniors, reminding us that we too can partner with God in carrying out His will and work even in our senior years.

Peter and John

The Bible suggests that both Peter and John lived long lives. The basis for this is found in the gospel of John, chapter 21. Prior to the crucifixion of Jesus, Peter had denied knowing Him three times. However, following Jesus' resurrection, Peter and John experienced a life-changing reunion with Jesus. John 21:18 predicts Peter's death as an old man.

Following Peter's declaration of love for Jesus, our Lord said, "Truly, truly, I say to you, when you were younger, you used to gird yourself, and walk wherever you wished: but when you grow old, you will stretch out your hands, and someone else will gird you, and bring you where you do not wish to go" (John 21:18 NIV). With these words, Jesus indicated the type of death Peter would experience (John 21:19).

Peter then asked about the future of the disciple John, and was bluntly told, "What is that to you? You follow Me" (John 21:22). The narrative implies that Peter and John, in spite of dying in different ways, served the early church as seniors.

The Apostle Paul

In all probability, Paul lived a relatively long life. Writing to Philemon concerning the restoration of his runaway slave, Onesimus, Paul says, "I rather appeal to you—since I am such a person as Paul, the aged, and now also a prisoner of Christ Jesus" (Philemon 9 NASB). Some think Paul spoke of himself as aged to enlist the sympathy of Philemon. I prefer to accept it for what it says.

Occasionally, Paul spoke of himself as a spiritual father to his converts (1 Corinthians 4:14–16; 2 Corinthians 6:13; 1 Thessalonians 2:11–12). It's interesting to notice that the Bible speaks of seniors as assets to be honored rather than burdens to be borne. The New Testament presents aging as an opportunity to serve rather than a fate to endure.

In chapter 1 I featured the world-famous Dr. Michael De-Bakey as a stellar role model. At age ninety-eight he was still serving. Earlier in this chapter, I shared about my boyhood pastor as my personal role model. However, there are hundreds of others. I would be remiss not to mention Billy Graham. He has modeled integrity, humility, compassion, and a continued involvement to this very day, despite his advanced age.

I first met and heard Billy at a Chicago youth rally in 1945. He inspired me then even as he inspires me to this very day. His body may be weak but his spirit is powerful. He has modeled the challenge of Paul to all: "My dear brothers, stand firm. Let nothing move you. Always give yourselves fully to the work of the Lord, because you know that your labor in the Lord is not in vain" (1 Corinthians 15:58).

And what about George Beverly Shea, still serving and

singing at age ninety-nine? Role models are all around, urging us not to die, 'til we die . . . but to *stay fresh and green,* to "still bear fruit in old age" (Psalm 92:14).

Faith is a . . . form of knowledge
which transcends the intellect.

—MALCOLM MUGGERIDGE

꧅

Faith is a reasoning trust, a trust which reckons thoughtfully
and confidently upon the trustworthiness of God.

—JOHN STOTT

꧅

My faith has no bed to sleep upon but omnipotence.

—SAMUEL RUTHERFORD

꧅

Faith is the refusal to panic.

—D. MARTYN LLOYD-JONES

꧅

Faith, mighty faith, the promise sees,
And looks to God alone;
Laughs at impossibilities,
And cries, it shall be done.

—CHARLES WESLEY

꧅

Attempt something so impossible that
unless God is in it, it's doomed to failure.

—JOHN E. HAGGAI

Chapter 9

THE CALEB
SECRET

By any standard, Caleb of the Old Testament lived a long, successful life. Even a casual review of his life reveals three longevity traits. First, Caleb was famous for his faith. He was an eighty-five-year-old optimist. Second, he kept fully involved in a giant cause for a lifetime. Third, he was connected to an extended family, tribe, and nation.

This chapter highlights Caleb's contagious faith. We first met Caleb when twelve representatives of the twelve tribes were chosen to spy out the land of Canaan (Numbers 13:2). Leaders were selected from each tribe for this strategic assignment. Caleb was chosen to represent the largest and most important tribe of Judah (Numbers 13:6). His selection speaks volumes concerning his ability and dedication.

The children of Israel had been in bondage in Egypt for more than four hundred years. Then Moses led them out through the Red Sea and across the wilderness. Finally, more than a million Israelites arrived at the border town of Kadesh Barnea. With the Promised Land before them, they could either occupy it in faith or retreat in unbelief.

After a forty-day search of the land, the twelve spies returned with their findings.

THE MAJORITY REPORT

All twelve leaders agreed that the land was special. They said it flowed with milk and honey. But ten reported, *"Nevertheless* the *people* who dwell in the land are *strong;* the cities are fortified and very large; *moreover* we saw the descendants of Anak there" (Numbers 13:28, italics added). The majority report of the ten turned on two well-worked words of doubt and defeat . . . *nevertheless* and *moreover.* The challenge is appealing; nevertheless, the difficulties are great; moreover . . .

There was an element of truth in what they said. The cities would not surrender without a tough fight, and the Anaks were big. However, in their fear, they *magnified* the problems.

Pandemonium broke loose, and the people "wept that night" (Numbers 14:1). The negative attitude of the ten spies spread like a wildfire, engulfing the whole nation. However, there were two other voices yet to be heard.

THE MINORITY REPORT

Ten spies brought back a pessimistic story. But Caleb and Joshua possessed an amazing faith. They challenged the people, "Let us go up at once and take possession, for we are well able to overcome it" (Numbers 13:30).

Why the differences? The ten and the two were describing the same situation. The difference was that Caleb and Joshua included God in the picture. They said, "If the Lord delights in us, that's what really matters." In the light of God's ability, the difficulties melted to a reasonable size.

Caleb and Joshua focused on divine ability, while the ten

looked at the land and its inhabitants. Their reports were totally different because their attitudes were totally different.

It was not just the walled cities that made the spies throw up their hands. It was not even their enemies' stature and strength. It was the spies' faulty relationship. "They have not wholly followed Me" (Numbers 32:11). They had no heart to follow. What they *were* not determined what they *did* not.

Their separation from God, first, *affected their attitude toward the land.* We are told they "have despised [it]" and brought "up a slander upon" it (Numbers 14:31, 36 KJV).

Their lack of faith also determined *their attitude toward the inhabitants.* Because the ten spies could not see God, they saw giants. Panic overwhelmed them, and fear snuffed out whatever faith they had. It's also revealing to see how their faithless attitude twisted the way they saw themselves. "There we saw the giants" (the descendents of Anak came from the giants), they told the people, "and we were like grasshoppers in our own sight, and so we were in their sight" (Numbers 13:33).

They saw themselves as grasshoppers because instead of looking to God they focused on the giants who opposed them. It's always that way when we minimize God. The obstacles seem huge.

In their own sight they were as grasshoppers, but what were they in God's sight? They were His chosen. He had shattered Egypt for them and defeated Amalek and others who had opposed them. Every promise He had kept, but now the past was forgotten.

ATTITUDE DETERMINES ACTION

Your attitude can work against you, but Caleb's life shows how it can also work for you. That's how it was with Caleb and Joshua.

Six times in Numbers, Deuteronomy, and Joshua, we read

concerning Caleb, "He wholly followed the Lord." This tells the secret of success. What Caleb was determined what Caleb did. His attitude determined his actions!

Caleb was an overcomer, because he had committed his entire life to God. Caleb and Joshua described the land as "an exceedingly good land" (Numbers 14:7). Earlier, Caleb had urged the people to "go up at once and take possession" (Numbers 13:30).

His was the reasoning of faith. God had promised the land to the people. He had said it was theirs, that He would go with them to receive it. Caleb believed. Going against the crowd took courage. A million angry people were ready to stone him. But the majority was wrong, and Caleb was right.

Notice Caleb's attitude toward the people of Canaan. True, they were like giants, but he had placed his faith in God. "They are our bread," he told his countrymen (Numbers 14:9). That sounds something like, "They're a piece of cake."

Caleb wasn't wearing rose-colored glasses. The enemies were big and tough, but beyond them, Caleb saw the supernatural. His faith was larger than his fear.

Consider Caleb's attitude toward God. "If the Lord delights in us," he said, "then He will bring us into this land" (Numbers 14:8). He knew God's promise and believed it.

God said, "Possess the land." Unbelief said, "We can't." But Caleb saw the difficulties as opportunities to display supernatural power.

Notice Caleb's attitude toward himself. His was not an arrogant stance. He did not rely on his own ability. He saw himself linked in a unique partnership. "If the Lord delights in us," he reasoned, "then we shall succeed." Caleb knew his power was not in himself.

Why was Caleb successful?

1. Caleb desired Canaan; the ten despised it.
2. Caleb sought to enter the land; the ten slandered the land.
3. Caleb had the spirit of a winner; the ten had the spirit of losers.
4. Caleb looked up at God's promise; the others looked in at themselves and around at their enemies.
5. Caleb saw God; the ten saw giants.
6. Caleb wholly followed the Lord; the ten set Him aside.

How is it with you? Do you face a crucial decision, a Kadesh Barnea that may change the course of your future? The land to claim or the giants to fight in your life may be unspectacular, but significant nonetheless. It may be a difficult circumstance to accept, a work to be undertaken, a burden to be borne, a victory to be claimed.

Remember Caleb's secret. Don't be misled by circumstances or frightened by difficulties. They're not what matters. It is your *attitude* that counts.

It's a megamistake to worry about obstacles when the Omnipotent is involved. Caleb won the battles of life because *he first won the battle of faith*. That was Caleb's secret . . . and it can be yours.

Fear makes the wolf bigger than he is.

—GERMAN PROVERB

―――

Fear knocked at the door. Faith answered. No one was there.
Good-bye, proud world! I'm going home.

—RALPH WALDO EMERSON

―――

God's finger touched him, and he slept.

—ALFRED, LORD TENNYSON

―――

Today I entered on my eighty-second year and found
myself just as strong to labor and as fit for any
exercise of body or mind as I was forty years ago.

—JOHN WESLEY

Chapter 10

NOTHING TO FEAR . . . BUT FEAR ITSELF

I shall always remember the words of President-elect Franklin D. Roosevelt, March 4, 1933. Because President Roosevelt had been paralyzed from polio fourteen years earlier, his son James helped his father stand to receive the oath of office. Despite the chilly wind, the president stood hatless and coatless, seeking to convey strength despite his personal disability.

The United States had struggled through four years of severe depression and ached for a ray of hope. To the thousands gathered on the Capitol steps and the millions listening by radio, Roosevelt confidently began, "Let me assert my firm belief, that the only thing we have to fear . . . is fear itself—nameless, unreasoning, unjustified terror paralyzes the needed efforts to convert retreat . . . into advance." That day, his sheer faith and charisma energized the nation to overcome its fears.

Again, on September 11, 2001, our nation was paralyzed by fear when the Pentagon in Washington and the Twin Towers in New York City were attacked by terrorists. On November 1, 2001, Rick Hampton wrote in *USA Today*: "Fear is a weapon. It is the knife that would sever our faith in each other, the club that would beat us into resignation, the gun that would stop us from flying. . . . Fear would make us hoard antibiotics and seek needless tests . . . it would make us shun skyscrapers . . . it would induce a national nervous breakdown. But those who study fear agree: Frightening civilians . . . is a loser's hand."[1]

Fear knows every age group. Some are afraid to go to the supermarket even in broad daylight. Others are afraid the next phone call will bring bad news concerning the children or grandchildren. Sick people are afraid of what the doctor may discover during their next checkup. And thousands more are afraid their money will run out. Fear is without doubt the enemy of every age.

Fear, like a drop of ink in a glass of water, discolors everything. Fear ties people in knots. It paralyzes thinking and acting. It can make life a living death.

Not long ago, a group of scholars expressed their thoughts about the next fifty years. One scientist predicted a person born today would live to be one hundred years old. During that time they will probably see the world run out of oil and natural gas. They will live through a period of drought and worldwide famine. They would also live through a nuclear attack that would level a major city.

WHAT IS FEAR?

Fear is a "painful emotion marked by alarm, or dread." It is a response to what we think will be unpleasant. Fear is as old as the world. Of course, not all fear is bad. The fear that prevents a person from stepping into a busy street may save a life. The fear that keeps us from touching a high-voltage wire or driving through a stoplight is lifesaving. Psychologists tell us four basic fears plague people:

1. The Fear of Want

It is common and even normal to indulge in the "what-if" game. "What if I get sick, and my bills exceed my ability to pay?" "What if the country goes into a depression, and the stock market fails?" Are these legitimate fears? First, these are unlikely fears. Most of what we fear never happens. Second, for the person of faith—now brace yourself—these fears are not valid. Why? Because ultimately God is the Provider. The issue is stated clearly in the Sermon on the Mount: "If God so clothes the grass of the field, which today is, and tomorrow is thrown into the oven, will He not much more clothe you, O you of little faith?" (Matthew 6:30).

Can you believe in God's ability to supply your needs? I find great strength in the words of David, "I have been young, and now am old; yet I have not seen the righteous forsaken, nor his descendents begging bread" (Psalm 37:25). Occasionally I quote, "The Lord is my shepherd; I shall *not want*" (Psalm 23:1, italics added).

2. The Fear of Suffering

Do you fear suffering? This could be pain of body or spirit. We tend to fear sickness, loneliness, and grief. Suffering is part of living. God doesn't shield us from suffering but rather controls it for our advantage.

A friend of mine was seriously injured in a highway accident. She spent many pain-filled months recovering. But during those months she grew more spiritually than in all her previous years. Today she looks back at her suffering as the most important and valuable experience of her lifetime. Suffering can be an opportunity to get to know God and ourselves better. Paul wrote, "My grace is sufficient for you, for my power is made perfect in weakness" (2 Corinthians 12:9 NIV).

3. The Fear of Failure

A common kind of fear is of failure. We want to be liked. We want to be accepted and included, especially if we've lost a loved one or friend and we're alone. Regarding loneliness, we need to be a friend to others rather than waiting for others to reach out to us. This requires thoughtfulness and a conscious effort to help others.

For the person of faith, the ultimate concern is to seek God's will and do it. The heroes of faith listed in Hebrews 11 were people who believed God and gave themselves to fulfill His will.

Here's a formula for overcoming the fear of failure: "Do not let this Book of the Law depart from your mouth; meditate on it day and night, so that you may be careful to do everything written in it. Then you will be prosperous and successful" (Joshua 1:8 NIV).

4. The Fear of Death

Is life harder toward the end? Not necessarily. Granted, there are at times severe physical limitations, but they are balanced by the luxury of free time and the chance to pursue our passions of life. The slower pace is a treat. I enjoy each day as a time to walk, visit, read, see friends, and do good for others. The last chapter of life can be like an autumn day with a full harvest and colorful leaves. There's nothing quite like a clear, fall day.

And yet some people are fearful of death. For people of faith, death is called "the valley of the shadow of death" (Psalm 23:4). The shadow of a dog can't bite. The shadow of a gun can't kill. Because of the resurrection, death has been robbed of its sting and is just a shadow (1 Corinthians 15). "How strange this fear of death is! We are never frightened at a sunset," writes George MacDonald.

The great musician Wolfgang Mozart lived a short life,

dying at the age of thirty-five. At age seven he sang, composed, and played the harpsichord, the organ, and the violin, winning acclaim throughout Austria. At age thirty he wrote to his father Leopold:

> Since death is the true end and purpose of our life, I have made it my business over the past few years to get to know this true, this best friend of man so well that the thought of him not only holds no terror for me, but even brings me great comfort and peace of mind. I thank my God that He has granted me the good fortune and opportunity to get to know death as the key to our true happiness. I never go to bed without reflecting on the thought that perhaps, as young as I am, the next day I might not be alive any more. And no man who knows me well will be able to say that in social intercourse I am morose or sad. For this happiness I thank every day my Creator, and with all my heart I wish this happiness for all my fellowmen.[2]

Several years ago I invited several senior leaders to Chicago to honor them for a life of outstanding service to the church and mankind. After I read a glowing tribute to Theodore Epp of Lincoln, Nebraska, he addressed our faculty and students. He began, "This is the last sermon I will ever deliver. I have come here to finish my work, where you are beginning yours." I was startled by his opening remarks, and yet I was soon caught up in his challenge. At the close, hundreds of students asked me what he meant by his opening sentence. "I don't have a clue," I answered.

At the end of the day, Dr. Epp flew to Lincoln, Nebraska, and arrived safely. The next morning he entered the hospital for a physical checkup and never left the hospital. It was indeed his last sermon. Theodore Epp lived and died by faith.

On another occasion, Herbert Lockyer, age ninety-seven, was able to come and be honored for a lifetime of speaking and writing. His mind was sharp and his voice was full, though his body bore the marks of aging. Two students assisted him to the podium. Once there, the adrenaline flowed, and he was magnificent. Coming to the close he said, "I'm not looking for the undertaker. I'm looking for the uppertaker." As he sat down next to me on the platform, he leaned over and whispered, "Did I hit the ball out of the park?" "Yes, you did. You surely did," I replied.

Though the unknown has its difficult moments, for people of faith, fear can be displaced by trust. "When I am afraid, I will trust in you" (Psalm 56:3 NIV).

UP-HILL

Does the road wind up-hill all the way?
Yes, to the very end.
Will the day's journey take the whole long day?
From morn to night my friend.

But is there for the night a resting-place?
A roof for when the slow dark hours begin,
May not the darkness hide it from my face?
You cannot miss that inn.

Shall I meet other wayfarers at night?
Those who have gone before.
Then must I knock, or call when just in sight?
They will not keep you standing at that door.

Shall I find comfort, travel-sore and weak?
Of labor you shall find the sum.
Will there be beds for me and all who seek?
Yea, beds for all who come.

—CHRISTINA ROSSETTI[3]

The only safe rule is to give more than we can spare.
Our charities should pinch and hamper us.
If we live at the same level of affluence as other
people who have our level of income,
we are probably giving away too little.

—C. S. Lewis

God does not need our money.
But you and I need the experience of giving it.

—James C. Dobson

Money reveals where our interests lie; it can direct
our attitudes; it ever exposes us to the danger
of worshiping it; and it represents value.
Money not only talks, "it screams."

—Leslie B. Flynn

Human worth does not lie in riches or power, but in
character or goodness. . . . If people would only
begin to develop this goodness. . . . Give of yourself. . . .
You can always give something, even if it is only Kindness. . . .
No one has ever become poor from giving.

—Anne Frank

———

The voyage of my life at last has reached,
Across a stormy sea, in a fragile boat,
The common port all must pass through, to give
An accounting for every evil and pious deed.
So now I recognize how laden with error
Was the affectionate fantasy
That made art an idol and sovereign to me
Like all things men want in spite of their best interests.
What will become of all my thoughts of love,
Once gay and foolish, now that I'm nearing two deaths?
I'm certain of one thing, and the other looms over me.
Neither painting nor sculpture will be able any longer
To calm my soul now turned toward that divine love
That opened his arms on the cross to take us in.

—Michelangelo (Florentine Italian, 1475–1564)

———

Seldom repress a generous impulse.

—George Sweeting

Chapter 11

DO YOUR GIVING WHILE YOU'RE LIVING

Giving is an essential part of being alive. Dead things may accumulate but they can't grow. Only living things . . . grow.

William Gladstone, the brilliant British statesman, said concerning giving, "There is no merit in a man leaving money in his will; he has simply got to leave it. The time to administer your trust . . . is while you are still living."

King Solomon was rich beyond any of his day. Yet in death, before his body had a chance to grow cold, the family was feuding over the distribution of his assets.

Do your giving while you're living. One benefit is the chance to see firsthand the good your giving can do. To see loved ones helped is especially rewarding. To enable struggling people to find hope provides enormous satisfaction.

THE SIN OF OLD AGE

While leading a seminar with seniors, I was asked, "What is the sin of old age?" That's a challenging question.

I began to answer by attempting to identify the primary sin of youth. I believe that the sin of youth is "the lust of the flesh," often referred to as "sex." Sex pervades most of life, from the books we read and the films we see to the selling of undergarments. Though sex appeals to all ages, it is aimed especially at youth.

During the middle years, many wrestle with the "pride of life." You can do it! Take care of yourself! Make it while you're hot; you stay cold a long time. Ego struts its stuff, while at the same time looking for security. Ego appears to be the sin of the middle years.

But what is the sin of old age? Greed. The accumulation of things. The quest for more. The push for security. Old age confuses *having* with *being*. However, what you *are* beats what you *have*, any day.

Another word for greed is "covetousness." Covetousness is an excessive desire for things. Covetousness is a megaproblem, so deceitful as to be linked with the grossest of crimes.

It was one of the first sins committed by the children of Israel when they entered the Promised Land. A man named Achan coveted silver, gold, and clothing and took it for himself despite Joshua's warning (Joshua 7).

The Ten Commandments warn against covetousness. "You shall not covet your neighbor's house. You shall not covet your neighbor's wife . . . or anything that belongs to your neighbor" (Exodus 20:17 NIV).

WHAT IS STEWARDSHIP?

Another benefit of "giving while you're living" is the opportunity to model good stewardship. A steward is one who manages the property of another. A steward lays aside all personal interest and thinks only of the welfare of the owner.

People of faith view all property as belonging to God and

ourselves as administrators. As stewards we need to be wise, honest, industrious, and, most of all, faithful.

Too often assets are given to children or friends without adequate guidance. Along with our giving, we can provide wise counsel. We can even give incrementally to observe how the gift is received and used.

John Wesley had a famous saying: "Get all you can, save all you can, give all you can." Dallas Willard suggests a modification: "Get all you can; save all you can; freely use all you can within a properly disciplined spiritual life, and control all you can for the good of humankind and God's glory. Giving all you can would then naturally be a part of an overall wise stewardship."[1]

All I have, including life itself, is a trust. Stewardship goes beyond my money and includes my body, mind, time, words, and deeds. Every person is a steward—whether he chooses to be or not. We are either good stewards or bad ones, but we cannot escape being one.

John D. Rockefeller Jr., businessman and philanthropist, said, "Giving is the secret to a healthy life. Not necessarily money, but whatever a person has to give of encouragement, sympathy, and understanding." An ancient proverb reminds us:

What I kept, I lost,
What I spent, I once had,
What I gave, I STILL have.

John Bunyan wrote in *The Pilgrim's Progress*: "A man there was, and they called him mad; the more he gave, the more he had."

Giving while you're living is a good way of knowing where it's going.

UNUSED MONEY

The *Wall Street Journal*, a paper devoted to the discussion of finance, described money as "an article which may be used as a universal passport to everywhere except Heaven, and as a universal provider of everything except happiness."

If money is to be useful . . . it must be used. Henry Ford said, "Money is like an arm or leg . . . you either use it or lose it."

The Dead Sea, in southern Israel, is a forty-seven-mile-long lake fed by the Jordan River. No animal life exists in its waters. It is the Dead Sea because it only takes in and never gives out.

The New Testament includes a poignant phrase about unused money. "The rust of [your riches] shall be a witness against you" (James 5:3 KJV). Rust speaks of disuse. It is a sure sign of inactivity.

Unused money will never clothe the cold or feed the hungry. Unused money will never heal the sick and lift the fallen. Unused money speaks of faulty stewardship. Unused money witnesses against us.

Of course, it is right and reasonable to retain sufficient money for the emergencies of life; however, a wise steward *uses* money wisely.

MISUSED MONEY

Keith Nicholson was an average mine worker when he won $500,000 in a British soccer pool. His wife, who never had money before, announced they were going to "spend, spend, spend." The Nicholsons bought a house, two cars, and several television sets. They began to give parties weekly. Before long they spent half of their newfound wealth. "We had oodles of money," reported Mrs. Nicholson, "and we set the place alight, but soon we lost our friends. The people we had known in the old days just stopped coming to see us."

Soon the Nicholsons lost all of their wealth, as well as their friends, largely because of misuse.

The way we use our money, over and above our needs, reveals a lot about us. The person who picks up the newspaper and immediately turns to the financial page probably has some money tied up in stocks and bonds. A large annual expenditure for clothing reveals a strong interest in personal appearance. It's true that where your dollars go is where your interests lie. "Where your treasure is, there your heart will be also" (Matthew 6:21).

A friend of mine gives generously to humanitarian causes, especially world missions. Recently, he was asked to report to the local Internal Revenue Service. When questioned about the large sums of money he reported as contributions, my friend produced his canceled checks as proof of his giving. The agent reviewed the checks, and when he was fully convinced that this man actually gave all the money he claimed to have given, he looked at him and said, "You certainly take your faith seriously."

WISELY USED MONEY

The way we give is also the way we receive. The New Testament book of Luke states it this way, "Give, and it will be given to you: good measure, pressed down, shaken together, and running over . . . for with the same measure that you use, it will be measured back to you" (6:38).

A measure was a unit like a pint, quart, or gallon. Some merchants were dishonest while others were stingy. The writer simply says, "The way you give is the way you will receive."

Early in life, I was taught the joys of giving. Even as a boy, often selling magazines, and later as a teenager working on a milk truck, I tithed 10 percent of my earnings (Malachi 3:10). When my wife and I launched our marriage fifty-five years ago, we agreed to begin giving a tithe of 10 percent and increase that amount as we prospered (1 Corinthians 16:2). Giving has brought us great joy.

Let me tell you about a man who used his money wisely. More than one hundred years ago, before the Quaker Oats Company existed, a group of millers in Ravenna, Ohio, banded together to change the breakfast menu of America. Until then, the familiar rolled oats we now drench in milk were fed almost exclusively to livestock. Moving those oats from feed silos to our breakfast bowls was a monumental job. The infant industry desperately needed someone with marketing and organizational know-how, and that someone was Henry Crowell.

Henry Crowell came from a well-to-do New England family that, despite its good fortune, was plagued by chronic tuberculosis. At age nine, young Henry stood at his father's grave, lonely and afraid.

After the pastor spoke the words of committal, young Henry asked to talk with him about life and death. The next day the two knelt in the minister's study as the boy decided to become a Christian.

At seventeen, Crowell himself was stricken with tuberculosis, which had killed four family members already. Doctors told young Crowell to quit school and forget his plans to attend college.

For two years, he rested and worked as a part-time show salesman in the firm his father founded. During those years, D. L. Moody spoke at their Cleveland church. Mr. Moody spoke about how God changed his life through the words of Henry Varley: "The world has yet to see what God can do with, and for, and through, a man who is fully and wholly consecrated to Him."

"Varley didn't say this person had to be educated," Moody testified that night, "or brilliant, or anything else! Just a person!"

Young Crowell thought, *I'll be one of those people!* With his new commitment, Crowell accepted his ruined school plans as confirmation that God didn't need a brilliant servant, just a yielded one.

Still, Crowell's health continued to deteriorate. The next year, in August 1874, he was told to quit his job and do nothing but rest.

Henry Crowell seriously studied his Bible during this time of poor health. He became fascinated by the frequent reference to the number seven. One night he read a passage in the book of Job. "He shall deliver thee in six troubles: yea, in seven there shall no evil touch thee" (Job 5:19 KJV).

He believed that the Lord was speaking to him, telling him he would not die at an early age. His faith grew as his condition became so critical that the doctors reevaluated his case and made a startling recommendation: "You have to live outdoors for the next seven years."

Crowell acted on the doctors' recommendation and went west to the Dakotas to regain his health. Often he experienced loneliness, especially when his fiancee's mother, believing he was dying, persuaded her daughter to break their engagement. But it wasn't God's will for him to die. Instead, Crowell slowly regained his health.

By the fourth year, he began to use his business sense to buy and sell farmland in South Dakota. But during the last year of his exile, a dry spell shriveled his wheat crop from twenty-five bushels per acre to eleven.

Is God moving me from farming? Crowell wondered. Within days, a man offered to buy his prizewinning Percheron horses, as well as his land, allowing Crowell to return to Cleveland. "I felt that I was not in good health," he wrote, "but I would wait and see what God would do next. I knew He would show me what He wanted."

Within thirty days of the sale, a man offered to sell Crowell a Quaker's mill at Ravenna, Ohio. "I doubt if it will make a success," the man admitted. But Crowell thought differently. As early as 1882, Mr. Crowell outlined a plan for his newly acquired mill: "To make better oatmeal than has ever been made, and to combine such companies as are interested and willing into a chartered company."

Crowell's plans were big: "The general company should displace old names with a single trade marker. To this end, it must do educational work, and create an oat demand where none exists. It is only by such a broad distribution and central management that we can avoid the perils of panic, competition, or disaster to some one plant or other."

His plan was so innovative that it took him twenty-five years to convince the small mill owners to give up their petty rivalries and organize under the Quaker Oats Company. Those were twenty-five years of patient waiting and gentle determination.

In 1888, the Crowell family came under the teaching of William R. Newell. His teaching revolutionized the lives of the Crowell family. At the same time, the Quaker Oats Company was revolutionizing the world's breakfast habits. By 1910, Quaker became a world organization, the first American food processor to reach this pinnacle.

Once his fortune was made, Crowell became a businessman who believed "a man's business is not chiefly his way of making a living, but his altar where he serves."[2] His stewardship focused on three areas: his time, his money, and his social action. For more than forty years, he gave 65 percent of his income and a great deal of his time to Christian work. He used his money wisely.

The vow young Henry Crowell made lasted more than seventy years, until his death. At age fifty-five, Mr. Crowell wrote on his desk pad, "If my life can always be lived, so as to please Him, I will be superbly happy."

Crowell did most of his giving while living; however, he also established a trust that aids nonprofit organizations to this day. He wisely used his money.

> *Do your giving while you're living . . .*
> *Then you're knowing where it's going!*

Lord, grant that my last hour may be my best hour.

—OLD ENGLISH PRAYER

If we really think that home is elsewhere and that
this life is a "wandering to find home,"
why should we not look forward to the arrival?

—C. S. LEWIS

Death is the great adventure beside which moon landings
and space trips . . . pale into significance.

—JOSEPH BAYLY

So he passed over, and all the trumpets
sounded for him . . . on the other side.

—JOHN BUNYAN, from *The Pilgrim's Progress*

In the theological phrase we "make up our souls"; this is the great achievement that makes death the completion of something that has become a unity, with a quality of accomplishment and significance for ourselves and those around us. This is what makes age not a burden and a defeat, but marvelously enjoyable in spite of the limitations of the aging body.

—Wayne Booth

Happy and wise are those who endeavor to be during this life . . .as they wish to be found at their death. Apply yourself so to live now, that at the hour of death, you may be glad and unafraid.

—Thomas À Kempis

A man I know found out last year he had terminal cancer. He was a doctor and knew about dying, and he didn't want to make his family and friends suffer through that with him. So he kept his secret. And died. Everybody said how brave he was to bear his suffering in silence and not tell anybody. But privately his family and friends said how angry they were that he didn't need them, didn't trust their strength. And it hurt that he didn't say good-bye.

—Robert Fulghum

Chapter 12

FINISHING
WITH GRACE

Dying is something we all have to do. But how well do we do it?

My predecessor, William Culbertson, served as the fifth president of Chicago's famed Moody Bible Institute. Occasionally he would tell the students that he prayed he would live his life in such a way that he could "die well."

I was privileged to work with him and to watch him live out his final days. I had the honor of being his pastor and serving as a trustee under his leadership. In 1971, I learned he was struggling with lung cancer. However, outwardly, he appeared quite vigorous, and I felt that with medical care and divine intervention he would recover. Early in 1971, the trustee board asked if I would succeed him as president. In summer 1971, his physical condition declined rapidly, yet neither his family nor friends felt that his death was imminent.

September was particularly difficult for him. On October 6, he entered the Swedish Covenant Hospital for a series of treatments. The cancer advanced with vengeance, making each day increasingly difficult. On the day of his death, November 16, he shared a favorite verse with several, "Alleluia! For the Lord God Omnipotent reigns!" (Revelation 19:6). However, none of us, as I recall, felt this was the last day of his life. After the visitors left, shortly before midnight, he spoke quietly as though he were speaking directly to his Maker, "God, God—yes!" With that, he closed his eyes in death. His prayer was answered; he died well and he finished with grace.

I too desire to die well, and if possible to help my loved ones and friends die well too.

ENDING WELL

Francis of Assisi, the thirteenth-century Italian evangelist, lived a modest life of poverty even though he was the son of a wealthy textile merchant. His final days were remarkable. Francis asked his doctor how long he could expect to live. When told that his condition was incurable and death would soon arrive, Francis, with great joy, raised his hands to welcome death. After bidding farewell to family and friends, he wrote a few letters. Sensing the end was near, he asked his doctor to announce the arrival of death. Said Francis, "Death will open the door of life," and then he softly quoted Psalm 142:7, "Bring my soul out of prison, that I may praise Your name." He struggled to sing:

> Death is our sister, we praise You for Death
> Who releases the soul to the light of Your gaze;
> And dying we call with the last of our breath
> Our thanks . . . and our praise.

Francis died . . . singing!

William Blake, the eighteenth-century artist/poet, is heralded as one of England's greatest. His father, a London stocking maker, recognized his son's talent and enrolled him at age ten in art study. From the start Blake displayed strong mystical tendencies, which eventually dominated his life's work.

Blake enjoyed a remarkable marriage to Catherine Boucher. On the day of his death, he called for Catherine to sit beside him and said, "Kate, you have been a good wife; I will draw your portrait." As she sat by his bedside, he sketched and sang with great joy, songs of triumph and hallelujahs. He rejoiced because as he was dying he sensed that he had "fought a good fight" and finished the race and soon would achieve the goal.

Just before he died, his face glowed, his eyes sparkled, and he began to sing about what he saw in heaven. Blake died well.

A contemporary, Willie Mae Smith, exclaimed as death approached, "I'm getting ready to go. How am I doing it? I'm laying aside every weight and sin that does so easily beset me . . . and I'm getting light for the flight."

For people of faith, death is an experience to prepare for and befriend. Henry Nouwen asks, "Can we wait for our death as for a friend who wants to welcome us home?"[1]

LIFE'S CERTAINTY

In life we prepare for many contingencies; however, "death" is not a contingency but a certainty. Birth and death circle us, like a challenging moat.

Novelist Somerset Maugham tells of an Arabian merchant who sent his servant to the city of Baghdad to buy provisions. While in the marketplace, the servant saw Death, who appeared to point at him. In panic, the servant fled to tell his master of the encounter. He asked for the use of a horse so he could escape to the distant town of Samara.

Later that day, the merchant also visited the Baghdad marketplace. Seeing Death he asked, "Why did you make a threatening gesture at my servant this morning?" Death answered, "That wasn't a threatening gesture, but rather a start of surprise.

I was astonished to see him here in Baghdad because tonight I have an appointment with him in the far-off town of Samara."

Alan Seeger (1888–1919), a Harvard graduate and poet, enlisted in the French Legion during World War I. He wrote this poem almost two years before he was mortally wounded on July 4, 1919. Alan Seeger anticipated his personal appointment with death.

I HAVE A RENDEZVOUS WITH DEATH

I have a rendezvous with Death,
At some disputed barricade,
When Spring comes back with rustling shade
And apple-blossoms fill the air—
I have a rendezvous with Death

When Spring brings back blue days and fair.
It may be he shall take my hand
And lead me into his dark land
And close my eyes and quench my breath—

It may be I shall pass him still.
I have a rendezvous with Death
On some scarred slope of battered hill,
When Spring comes round again this year
And the first meadow-flowers appear.

God knows 'twere better to be deep
Pillowed in silk and scented down,
Where love throbs out in blissful sleep,
Pulse nigh to pulse, and breath to breath,
Where hushed awakenings are dear—

But I've a rendezvous with Death
At midnight in some flaming town,
When Spring trips north again this year,
And I to my pledged word am true,
I shall not fail the rendezvous.[2]

—ALAN SEEGER, 1916

In earlier days people lived with dying in mind, whereas today death is the great unmentionable. Psychologists claim the majority of people refuse to face death, even to the point of neglecting a yearly physical checkup, lest they confront their own mortality.

People face death differently. One dies in confidence, while another dies in doubt. Some die rejoicing, while others experience remorse. It was said that when King Jehoram died, "he departed *with no one's regret*" (2 Chronicles 21:20 NASB, italics added). He died wrong because he lived wrong. However, the Scripture says of Abijah that at his death "all Israel mourned for him" (1 Kings 14:18). In spite of heredity and environment, Abijah died right.

TWO WORDS FOR DEATH

For people of biblical faith there are two descriptive words in the Bible regarding death. In 2 Peter 1:15, the word translated "decease" is the Greek word *exodus*, the title of the second book of the Bible. It means, "the road out." The death of those of faith is a triumphant exodus . . . like the children of Israel released from the enslavement of Egypt. Death for the believer is a "going out" into God's presence. In Philippians 1:23, the apostle Paul wrote of his "desire to depart and be with Christ, which is far better" than earthly life. The Greek word translated *depart* means "to loose." The picture is of an anchor being lifted, freeing the boat to sail beyond the horizon into the unseen harbor. Death for those of faith is literally an "anchors aweigh." Malcolm Muggeridge speaks of death with joyful anticipation:

> So, like a prisoner awaiting his release, like a school-boy when the end of the term is near, like a migrant bird ready to fly south, like a patient in the hospital anxiously scanning the doctor's face to see whether a discharge may be expected, I long to be gone. Extricating myself from the flesh I have too long inhabited, hearing the key turn in the lock of time so that the great doors of eternity swing open, disengaging my tired mind from its interminable conundrums, and my tired ego from its wearisome insistencies. Such is the prospect of death.

ANCHORS FOR AGING

Paul the apostle suggests three anchors for aging that hold us steady in the face of death. In full confidence, Paul reminds the Corinthian church of the resurrection of Jesus: "Because we know that the one who raised the Lord Jesus from the dead will also raise us with Jesus" (2 Corinthians 4:14 NIV). Paul was positive of a future resurrection. He saw in the resurrection both the pattern and promise of the resurrection of each believer. It was his anchor in the storms of life.

Several years ago, a close family friend named Beverly was dying from cancer. From the beginning she reflected a radiant spirit not for healing, but for dying. She had befriended death. On one occasion she showed my wife and me her proposed funeral service under the caption, "My Praise Service." She had carefully selected the Scriptures to be read and the songs to be sung. She requested a period of time reserved for any in the audience to share in a voluntary, impromptu way, whatever they wanted to share.

On one occasion I tried to comfort her husband, Alan, as-suring him of our prayers and friendship. To which he replied, "George, if Bev were going to Hawaii, wouldn't you be happy for her?"

"Yes, of course," I answered.

"Well, heaven is a whole lot better than Hawaii."

Beverly's faith was anchored to the resurrection (2 Corinthi-ans 4:14). The confidence of a future gave Beverly a hope-filled perspective. This is an anchor for aging.

D. L. Moody, while speaking to a large New York City gath-ering, said, "Someday you will read in the papers that Moody is dead. Don't you believe a word of it. At that moment I shall be more alive than I am now. . . . I was born of the flesh in 1837, I was born of the Spirit in 1855. That which is born of the flesh will die. That which is born of the Spirit shall live forever." How could a person be so confident? Only because of confi-dence in a future resurrection.

The second anchor for aging is "an eternal glory that far outweighs them all" (2 Corinthians 4:17 NIV). It is the joy of living day by day in such a way as to lay up eternal treasure. It is to live with our gaze on eternity as well as time.

Missionary Amy Carmichael discovered this lifetime anchor as a teenager. Following a regular Sunday morning worship service, she met an elderly street woman carrying what seemed like an incredible bundle. Without a second thought, she of-fered to help the woman, only to recoil at what she thought others might think of her. However, in that moment, Amy Carmichael recalled the words of Scripture: "Gold, silver, pre-cious stones, wood, hay, straw. . . . If anyone's work . . . en-dures" (1 Corinthians 3:12–14). Though everything seemed quite ordinary, Amy knew that, in that moment, the values of her life had totally changed. From that day on, only that which was eternal . . . ultimately mattered. For over fifty years, she gave herself to rescue and care for hundreds of children sold to the gods as temple prostitutes in southern India. Amy Carmichael lived her life with "eternal glory" in view. Second Corinthians 4:1, 16 urges us to live out our lives with confidence, "and *not* lose heart."

Paul's third anchor for aging is "an eternal house in heaven, not built by human hands" (2 Corinthians 5:1 NIV). The apostle compares our earthly bodies to a "tent." At our very best, we're *frail*. A tent is temporal and an apt metaphor for our bodies. However, at the moment of death, our earthly bodies will be *replaced* with an eternal, imperishable body (1 Corinthians 15:42, 53–54). We have "an eternal house in heaven, not built by human hands." This is a megalife-changing anchor!

Each passing year our children find it challenging to buy my wife and me a Christmas gift. Our needs are simple. Several years ago they purchased for me *The Oxford Book of Aging*. I think they were trying to tell me something. I enjoyed the book, especially the poetry. I was lifted and challenged by a poem by Sterling Brown, an African-American. His wife had just died, and he writes to her in the old Negro dialect, instructing her about a future eternal home.

> *Honey*
> *When de man*
> *Calls out de las' train*
> *You're gonna ride*
> *Tell him howdy.*
>
> *Gather up yo' basket*
> *An' yo' knittin' an' yo' things.*
> *An' go on up an' visit*
> *Wid frien' Jesus fo' a spell.*
> *Show Marfa*

How to make yo' green grape jellies,
An' give po' Lazarus
A passel of them Golden Biscuits.

Scald some meal
Fo' some righdown good spoonbread
Fo' Li'l box-plunkin' David.

An' sit aroun'
An' tell them Hebrew Chillen
All yo' stories . . .

Honey
Don't be feared of them pearly gates.
Don't go 'round to de back,
No mo' dataway
Not evah no mo'.

Let Michael tote yo' burden
 An' yo' pocketbook an' evahthing
'Cept yo' Bible,
While Gabriel blows somp'n
Solemn but loudsome
On dat horn of his'n.

Honey
Go straight on to de Big House,
An' speak to yo' God
Widout no fear an' tremblin'.
Then sit down
An' pass de time of day awhile.

Give a good talkin' to
To yo' favorite 'postle Peter,

An' rub the po' head
Of mixed-up Judas,
An' joke awhile wid Jonah.

Then, when you gits de chance,
Always rememberin' yo' raisin',
Let 'em know youse tired
Jest a mite tired.
Jesus will find yo' bed fo' you
Won't no servant evah bother wid yo' room.
Jesus will lead you
To a room wid windows
Openin' on cherry trees an' plum trees
Bloomin' everlastin'.

An' dat will be yours,
Fo' keeps,
Den take yo' time . . .
Honey, take yo' bressed time.[3]

—STERLING A. BROWN

J. I. Packer reminds us, "Dying well is one of the good works to which Christians are called, and He will enable us to serve Him, *to die well.*" We can finish with grace.

Chapter 13

LEAVING A LEGACY

T he word *legacy* usually refers to something handed down to us from the past. Often we think of a legacy in terms of material assets; however, our real legacy includes the sum and total of all we *are, say,* and *do.*

A legacy in Bible times was thought of as a parting blessing, much like Jacob's dying words to his twelve sons. After finishing his blessing, "he drew his feet up into the bed and breathed his last" (Genesis 49:28–33). Several of the Psalms suggest the idea of leaving a spiritual legacy. "One generation will commend your works to another; they will tell of your mighty acts" (Psalm 145:4 NIV).

It's important to tell our life's story for loved ones and friends. We need to verbalize what's really important to us, including our ultimate reason for living.

THE LEGACY OF PETER

As the apostle Peter approached his death, he shared his lifetime legacy. He wrote, "I will make every effort to see that after my departure [death] you will always be able to *remember* these things" (2 Peter 1:15 NIV, italics added). Peter also said, "it is right to refresh your memory" (2 Peter 1:13). Peter left a written legacy for all to read and ponder.

It's helpful to think of a legacy as our love letter to family and friends. This can be shared verbally or written out in detail.

Each of us will include different experiences. For me, it would have to include my family with all its special memories. I would have to include my conversion and call to ministry, guidelines for a good marriage, and the significant lessons of life.

OFFERING A BLESSING

The word *good-bye* comes from the phrase "God be with you." The word *good* is defined as morally excellent, virtuous, and righteous—words ultimately applicable only to God (Mark 10:18).

My friend Dr. John Dunlop, M.D., suggests that our "good-bye," our blessing before we depart, should include four areas.

1. "I love you."

Too often, we neglect to simply say, "I love you." Our words are important to life and healing. It is also true that our love can be expressed by our deeds (1 John 3:18) and yet nothing will ever take the place of simply saying, "I love you."

2. "Thank you."

All too often we take gratitude for granted. However, our thanks needs to be spoken. People need to hear often that they are valued, needed, and appreciated. Paul the apostle wrote, "give thanks in all circumstances" (1 Thessalonians 5:18 NIV).

3. *"Forgive me."*

Each of us has failed in some way in our relationships with family and friends. We need a forgiving spirit regardless of who was at fault. Again, the Scriptures urge us to "confess your sins to each other" (James 4:16).

4. *"I forgive you."*

I walked through a forest following a devastating fire. It seemed doubtful that anything survived. Yet one year later, nature covered all the scars in a lush mantle of green. As I beheld the change I prayed for a forgiving spirit.

An unforgiving spirit blocks God's forgiveness to us. Scripture exhorts us to "forgive whatever grievances you may have against one another. Forgive as the Lord forgave you" (Colossians 3:13 NIV). May I encourage you to make these four phrases a sincere part of your legacy.

The writing of this book has been for me an enormous privilege and pleasure. I also realize that I have so much more to learn and experience. However, I want to finish with a blessing to you the reader.

May you, like the character named "Christian" in John Bunyan's allegory *The Pilgrim's Progress*, find firm, solid "ground to stand upon." May you find that the river of death that you may fear is really "shallow."

My blessing for you is that you, like the apostle Paul, "may finish . . . with joy" (Acts 20:24).

EXCERPTS FROM JOHN BUNYAN'S
The Pilgrim's Progress

Now I further saw, *that betwixt them and the gate was a river; but there was no bridge to go over*, and the river was very deep. At the sight, therefore, of this river, the pilgrims were much stunned; but the men that went with them said, "You must go through" . . .

The pilgrims then, especially Christian, began to despond in his mind, and looked this way and that; but no way could be found by them by which they might escape the river. Then they asked the men *if the waters were all of a depth. They said, "No"; yet they could not help them in that case;* "for," said they, *"you shall find it deeper or shallower as you believe in the King of the place."*

Then they addressed themselves to the water; and, entering, Christian began to sink, and crying out to his good friend Hopeful, he said, "I sink in deep waters; the billows go over my head; *all His waves go over me. Selah."*

Then said the other, "Be of good cheer, my brother; I feel the bottom, and it is good." Then said Christian, "Ah! my friend, the sorrows of death have compassed me about; I shall not see the land that flows with milk and honey."

And with that, a great darkness and horror fell upon Christian, so that he could not see before him . . .

Hopeful, therefore, here had much ado to keep *his brother's* head above water; yea, sometimes he would be quite gone down, and then, ere a while, he would rise up again half dead. Hopeful would also *endeavor to comfort him, saying, "Brother, I see the gate, and men standing by to receive us";* but Christian would answer, "It is you, it is you they wait for: *you have been hopeful ever since I knew you."* "And so have you," said he to Christian. "Ah, brother," said he, "surely if I were right He would now arise to help me; but for my sins He hath brought me into this snare, and hath left me". . . .

Then I saw in my dream, that *Christian was in a muse awhile.* To whom also Hopeful added these words, *"Be of good cheer, Jesus Christ maketh thee whole." And with that, Christian brake out with a loud voice, "Oh, I see Him again; and He tells me, 'When thou passeth through the waters, I will be with thee;* and through the rivers, they shall not overflow *thee.'"*

Then *they both took courage,* and the enemy was, after all, *as still as stone,* until they were gone over. Christian, therefore, *presently found ground to stand upon;* and so it followed that the rest of the river *was but shallow. Thus they got over.*

Jude also offers his blessing with a promise of great joy. "To him who is able to keep you from falling and to present you before his glorious presence without fault and <u>with great joy</u> . . ." (Jude 24 NIV). Yes, you can age . . . with joy!

Chapter 14

GREAT QUOTATIONS ON AGING AND DYING

THE LIGHTER SIDE OF AGING

It's nice to be here; when you're
99 years old it's nice to be anywhere.

—GEORGE BURNS

A joyous occasion is never quite as
wonderful as when it becomes a memory.

—PRESIDENT JIMMY CARTER

Life begins at 40—but so do fallen arches, rheumatism,
faulty eyesight, and the tendency to tell a story
to the same person, three or four times.

—BILL FEATHER

Children are a great help. They are a comfort in your old age.
And they help you reach it faster too.

—ANONYMOUS

There are three ages to mankind: youth,
middle age, and . . . my, you're looking good.

—NELSON ROCKEFELLER

You can take no credit for beauty at 16. But if you are
beautiful at 60, it will be your soul's own doing.

—MARIE STOPES

He's so old . . . his blood type was discontinued.

—BILL DANA

Whatever poet, orator, or sage may say of it, old age is still
old age.

—SINCLAIR LEWIS

Old age is when you know all the answers
. . . but nobody asks you any questions.

—LAWRENCE J. PETER

I'm 65 and I guess that puts me in with the geriatrics,
but if there were fifteen months in every year, I'd only be 52.

—JAMES THURBER

Old friends are best. King James used to call for his
old shoes; they were the easiest for his feet.

—WAYNE BOOTH

[When David Ben-Gurion came out of retirement for the ninth
time, he was asked by an American why he bothered to retire.]
"It's like those 'going out of business' signs you see along
Seventh Avenue—a chance to unload stock he doesn't want,
hire a new staff and make a different contract with the union."

—DAVID BEN-GURION

Life is 10 percent what you make it and
90 percent how you take it.

—IRVING BERLIN

My grandfather would look through the
obituary columns and say to me,
"Strange isn't it, how everybody
seems to die in alphabetical order".

—JACKIE VERNON

If you are over the hill, why not enjoy the view?

—MACK MCGINNIS

By the time a man gets to greener
pastures he can't climb the fence.

—FRANK DICKSON

I'm not getting old. My mirror is just getting wrinkled.

—ANONYMOUS

When a man's friends begin to compliment him about looking
younger, he may be sure that they think, he is growing old.

—WASHINGTON IRVING

I will not make age an issue . . . I am not going to exploit
for political purposes my opponent's youth and inexperience.

—RONALD REAGAN
(At age 73 concerning his 56-year-old opponent, Walter Mondale)

SERIOUS QUOTATIONS ABOUT AGING

We believe that aging is not a reason for despair but a basis
for hope, not a slow decaying but a gradual maturing, not a
fate to be undergone but a chance to be embraced.

—HENRY J. M. NOUWEN AND WALTER GAFFNEY

Preparation for old age should begin not later than one's teens. A life which is empty of purpose until 65 will not suddenly become filled on retirement.

—ARTHUR MORGAN

People are anxious to save up financial means for old age; they should also be anxious to prepare a spiritual means for old age . . . wisdom, maturity, tranquility do not come all of a sudden when we retire.

—ABRAHAM JOSHUA HESCHEL

If a thing is old, it is a sign that it was fit to live. Old families, old customs, old styles survive because they are fit to survive. The guarantee of continuity is quality. Submerge the good in a flood of the new, and the good will come back to join the good that the new brings with it. Old-fashioned hospitality, old-fashioned politics, old-fashioned honor in business had qualities of survival. These will come back.

—ANONYMOUS

What if someone had decided that Pablo Picasso, Pablo Casals, or Michelangelo, still producing in their 80s and 90s, had "no future" when they became 70 years old?

—MARGARET C. ELWELL

Age should not have its face lifted, but it should rather teach the world to admire wrinkles as the etchings of experience and the firm line of character.

—RALPH BARTON PERRY

Old age is just as important and meaningful a part of God's perfect will as is youth. God is every bit as interested in the old as the young.

—J. O. SANDERS

Father Time is not always a hard parent, though he tarries for none of his children, often lays his hand lightly upon those who have used him well.

—CHARLES DICKENS

The later decades of life become the time for our capabilities to find an unscattered focus, and in this way increase the force of their concentrated worth.

—SHERWIN B. NULAND

DR. E. STANLEY JONES SUGGESTED THE FOLLOWING STEPS FOR CONTINUING GROWTH IN OLD AGE:

1. *Don't retire. Change your occupation . . . do something you have always wanted to do.*
2. *Learn something new every day.*
3. *Set yourself to be gracious to someone every day.*
4. *Don't let yourself grow negative; be positive.*
5. *Look around you for something for which to be grateful every day. Gratitude will become a settled habit.*
6. *Now that your bodily activities are slowing down, let your spiritual activities increase. Old age provides increased opportunity for prayer.*
7. *Keep laying up as the years come and go to "the good store" of which Jesus spoke. This "good store" is the depository of every thought, motive, action, attitude which we drop into the subconscious mind. It can be the deep subsoil into which we can strike our roots in old age and blossom at the end of a night-blooming cereus.*

—E. STANLEY JONES

Your manner of life now is already determining your life in those years of old age and retirement, without your realizing it even, and perhaps without your giving enough thought to it. One must therefore prepare oneself for retirement.

—PAUL TOURNIER

In order to make a success of old age, one must begin it earlier, and not try to postpone it as long as possible. In the middle of life we must stop to think, to organize our existence with an eye to a still distant future, instead of allowing ourselves to be entirely sucked into the professional and social whirl. It is then that it is important to give place little by little to less external activities, less technical and more cultural, which will survive the moment of retirement.

—PAUL TOURNIER

It is only logical that if God's will is good and acceptable and perfect (Romans 12:2), then complaining about it or rebelling against it is out. If God's will is acceptable, it must be accepted.

—J. O. SANDERS

ON WAKING IN PRISON
0 God, early in the morning I cry to You
Help me to pray
And to concentrate my thoughts on You:
I cannot do this alone.
In me there is darkness,
But with You there is light;
I am lonely, but You do not leave me;
I am feeble in heart, but with You there is help;
I am restless, but with You there is peace.
In me there is bitterness, but with You there is patience;
I do not understand Your ways,
But You know the way for me.

—DIETRICH BONHOEFFER (1906–1945)
While awaiting execution in a Nazi prison

DEATH

You haven't lost anything when you know where it is.
Death can hide but not divide.

—VANCE HAVNER

I'm not afraid to die. I'm looking forward to it. I know
the Lord has His arms wrapped around this big sparrow.

—ETHEL WATERS

Life is a hard fight, a struggle, a wrestling with the principle of
evil, hand to hand, foot to foot. Every inch of the way is
disputed. The night is given us to take breath, to pray, to drink
deep at the fountain of power. The day, to use the strength
which has been given us, to go forth to work with it till the
evening.

—FLORENCE NIGHTINGALE

Since General MacArthur made his famous statement,
"Old soldiers never die, they just fade away,"
interesting quotations have been proposed. Such as,
Old postmen never die, they just lose their Zip.
Old scoutmasters never die, they just smell that way.
Old deans never die, they just lose their faculties.
Old doctors never die, they just lose their patience.

—ANONYMOUS

Every man must do two things alone; he must
do his own believing and his own dying.

—MARTIN LUTHER

The measure of a life, after all, is not
its duration but its donation.

—CORRIE TEN BOOM

If you draw near the end in somber circumstances, remember that as a faithful child of God you await promotion. Who knows but that the brightest jewel in your crown is for that lonely afternoon and night when all seemed lost but you believed anyway. Remember John the Baptist in prison and John on Patmos and countless millions who have been on that road before you. Remember Mr. Fearing in Bunyan's immortal Pilgrim's Progress, who dreaded Jordan all his days. But when he reached it, the water was a record low, and he got across "not much above wet-shod. " The last chapter in life can be the best.

—Vance Havner

So now, from this mad passion which
made me take art for an idol and a king,
I have learnt the burden of error that it bore.
And what misfortune springs from man's desire . . .
the world's frivolities have robbed me
of the time that I was given for reflecting upon God.

—Michelangelo

As a well-spent day brings happy sleep,
so life well used brings happy death.

—Leonardo Da Vinci

Lord Jesus Christ,
You are the only source of health for the living, and You promise eternal life to the dying. I entrust myself to Your holy will. If You wish me to stay longer in this world, I pray that You will heal me of my present sickness. If You wish me to leave this world, I readily lay aside this mortal body, in the sure hope of receiving an immortal body which shall enjoy everlasting health. I ask only that You relieve me of pain, that whether I live or die, I may rest peaceful and contented.

—ERASMUS (1469–1536), *Book of Prayers*

What is dying? Just what it is to put off a garment. For the body is about the soul as a garment; and after laying this aside for a short time by means of death, we shall resume it again with more splendor.

—ST. JOHN CHRYSOSTOM (347–407), early Christian saint

Death always waits. The door of the hearse is never closed.

—JOSEPH BAYLY

God buries His workmen but carries on His work.

—CHARLES WESLEY

Because I could not stop for death
He kindly stopped for me;
The carriage held but just ourselves
And immortality.

—EMILY ELIZABETH DICKINSON

Christ taught an astonishing thing about physical death: not merely that it is an experience robbed of its terror but that as an experience it does not exist at all. To "sleep in Christ," like one that wraps the drapery of his couch about him, and lies down to pleasant dreams.

—WILLIAM CULLEN BRYANT

I don't know what your destiny will be, but one thing I know,
the only ones among you who will be really happy are
those who have sought and found how to serve.

—ALBERT SCHWEITZER

Don't allow yourself to feel old; don't give up your interest in
life; cultivate a hobby; have a game now and then with your
grandchildren, or someone else's; don't think about the end—
God has lovingly planned that, and you will be as unaware of
your passing out as you were of your coming.

—F. B. MEYER

THE OLD PLAYER

Call him not old, whose visionary brain
Holds o'er the past its undivided reign.
For him in vain the envious seasons roll
Who bears eternal summer in his soul.

—OLIVER WENDELL HOLMES

People are reluctant to talk about old age and death because
they are afraid of emotion, and they willingly avoid the things
they feel most emotional about, though these are the very
things they most need to talk about.

—PAUL TOURNIER

Christian faith . . . does not involve repressing one's anxiety in
order to appear strong. On the contrary, it means recognizing
one's weakness, accepting the inward truth about oneself,
confessing one's anxiety . . . and still to believe; that is to say
that the Christian puts his trust not in his own strength, but in
the grace of God.

—PAUL TOURNIER

I will say with Lorenzo de Medici that those who
do not hope for another life are always dead to this one.

—GOETHE

You needn't worry about not feeling brave. Our Lord didn't.
. . . Remember the scene in Gethsemane. How thankful I am
that when God became man, He did not choose to become a
man of iron nerves; that would not have helped weaklings like
you and me nearly so much.

—C. S. Lewis

NOTES

CHAPTER 1: LIGHTEN UP!

1. George Sweeting, *Who Said That?* (Chicago: Moody, 1994), 30.

2. Dr. David Weeks and Jamie James, *Secrets of the Super Young* (New York: Villard Books/Random House, 1998), 23–24.

3. Ibid.

4. Sherwin Nuland, *The Art of Aging* (New York: Random House, 2007), 76.

5. *Esquire*, March 2001, 143.

CHAPTER 2: PEOPLE OF FAITH TEND TO LIVE LONGER

1. Marilyn Elias, "Widow of Sept. 11 Hero Carries On; She Says God Has a Plan, and It Put Todd Beamer on Flight 93," *USA Today*, 21 November 2001, D13.

2. David Snowdon, Ph.D., *Aging with Grace* (New York: Bantam, 2001), 202.

3. Thomas T. Perls and Margery Hutter Silver, *Living to 100: Lessons in Living to Your Maximum Potential at Any Age* (New

York: Persens Books, 1999), 77.

4. Donald H. Kausler and Barry C. Kausler, *The Graying of America*, 2nd ed. (Champaign, IL: University of Illinois, 2001), 23–37.

5. Snowdon, *Aging with Grace*, 202.

6. Kausler and Kausler, *The Graying of America*, 340.

7. Dr. Herbert Benson, *Beyond the Relaxation Response* (New York: Berkley, 1985).

8. D. O. Moberg, *Aging and Spirituality* (Birmingham, NY: Haworth Pastoral Press, 2001), 67.

9. Dr. Andrew Weil, *Healthy Aging* (New York: Andrew A. Knopf, 2005), 95.

CHAPTER 3: TEMPLE KEEPING

1. Bill Cosby, *Time Flies* (New York: Bantam, 1988), 35–39.

2. Donald H. Kausler and Barry C. Kausler, *The Graying of America*, 2nd ed. (Champaign, IL: University of Illinois, 2001), 177.

3. Ibid., 59.

4. John W. Rowe and Robert L. Kahns, *Successful Aging* (New York: Pantheon Books, 1998).

5. Dale Carnegie, *How to Stop Worrying and Start Living* (New York: Pocket Books, 1984), 4.

6. John E. Haggai's book, *How to Win Over Worry* (Eugene, OR: Harvest House Publishers, 1997), is a superb resource on overcoming worry.

CHAPTER 4: THE AGE BOOM

1. Peter G. Peterson, *Gray Dawn* (New York: Time Books, 1999), 3.

2. Ibid., 1.

3. Jimmy Carter, *The Virtues of Aging* (New York: Time Books, 1998), 28.

CHAPTER 5: AGING WITH JOY

1. Morton Puner, *To the Good Long Life* (New York: Universe Books, 1974).
2. Anne Morrow Lindbergh, *Gift from the Sea* (New York: Random House, 1955), 35.

CHAPTER 6: ARTERIES PLUS ATTITUDE

1. Michael F. Roizen, M.D., *Real Age: Are You as Young as You Can Be?* (New York: Cliff Street Books, 1999), 59.

CHAPTER 7: WHY COMEDIANS LIVE SO LONG

1. Thomas T. Perls and Margery Hutter Silver, *Living to 100: Lessons in Living to Your Maximum Potential at Any Age* (New York: Basic Books, 1999), 72.
2. Leslie B. Flynn, *Serve Him with Mirth* (Grand Rapids: Zondervan, 1960), 14–15.
3. Ibid., 44.
4. Ibid., 19.

CHAPTER 8: ROLE MODELS FOR AGING

1. Cited in Stanley Hauerwas, Carol Bailey Stoneking, Keith G. Meador, and David Cloutier, eds., *Growing Old in Christ* (Grand Rapids: Eerdmans, 2003), 3.

CHAPTER 10: NOTHING TO FEAR . . . BUT FEAR ITSELF

1. Rick Hampton, "Fear As a Weapon: Terrorist Tactics Rarely Triumph; but Hijackings, Anthrax Scares and Other Threats Have Rattled Many in the Home of the Brave," *USA Today*, 1 November, 2001, Sec. 1A and 2A.
2. Alfons Deeken, *Growing Old* (New York: Paulist, 1972), 99.
3. Wayne Booth, *The Art of Growing Older* (New York: Poseidon Press, 1992), 275.

CHAPTER 11: DO YOUR GIVING WHILE YOU'RE LIVING

1. Dallas Willard, *The Spirit of the Disciplines* (New York: Harper-Collins, 1988), 217.

2. Richard E. Day, *A Christian in Big Business: The Life Story of Henry Parsons Crowell* (Chicago: Moody, 1954), 161.

CHAPTER 12: FINISHING WITH GRACE

1. Henry Nouwen, *Our Greatest Gift* (New York: HarperCollins, 1995), xiii.

2. Franklyn B. Snyder and Edward D. Snyder, *A Book of American Literature* (New York: MacMillan, 1935), 1096.

3. Thomas R. Cole and Mary C. Winkler, *The Oxford Book of Aging* (New York: Oxford, 1994), 18–19.

MEET ME AT THE WELL

Noted speaker and author Virelle Kidder recently found herself at the end of her rope following a year of crises with her children and her mother. The end of that rope led to the well of Living Water! What started out as a drought in her life became the impetus for drawing deep. Virelle's candid, and oft-times humorous, reflection on the power of the Living Water will lead women to a month-long time of refreshment. She encourages all women to *Meet Me at the Well.*

(Mp) MOODY PUBLISHERS.

1-800-678-8812 · MOODYPUBLISHERS.COM

STRENGTH
FOR THE JOURNEY

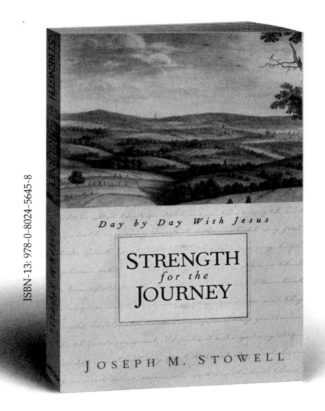

ISBN-13: 978-0-8024-5645-8

As the Christian experiences the ups and downs of this walk, a common prayer is "Lord, give me strength." Joseph Stowell presents this enriching devotional, overflowing with spiritual challenges, thought-provoking questions, and keen biblical insights. Six entries per week, plus a Psalm for the seventh day.

MOODY
PUBLISHERS.

1-800-678-8812 · MOODYPUBLISHERS.COM

A LIFE THAT MATTERS

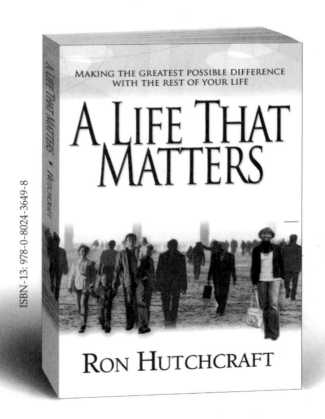

For the believer in Christ, lasting greatness is expected. How will your life count for eternity? God wants you to join the team of rescuers He is sending into a desperate world.